Sing to God

Songs and Hymns for Christian Education

Published for
Christian Education: Shared Approaches
by United Church Press
New York

Contents

2d printing, 1988

Sing to God: Songs and Hymns for Christian Education is published especially for use in the following denominations: American Baptist Churches USA, Christian Church (Disciples of Christ), Church of the Brethren, Cumberland Presbyterian Church, Friends General Conference, The Episcopal Church, Moravian Church in America, Presbyterian Church in Canada, The Presbyterian Church (U.S.A.), Reformed Church in America, and United Church of Christ.

All scripture quotations, unless otherwise indicated, are from the Revised Standard Version of the Holy Bible, Old Testament Section, copyright 1952; New Testament Section, Second Edition, copyright © 1971, 1973 by the Division of Christian Education of the National Council of Churches of Christ in the United States of America.

Editors: Mary Hawkes and Paul Hamill

Cover design and illustrations by Gloria Claudia Ortiz

Music Typography by AKRIT

United Church Press, 132 West Thirty-first Street, New York, NY 10001

Preface

SING TO GOD: SONGS AND HYMNS FOR CHRISTIAN EDUCATION has been developed to provide the church with a collection of quality songs and hymns of educational value for children, young people, and adults.

The idea for such a songbook originated from a consultation on the arts in Christian education sponsored by the Living the Word Resources Team of Christian Education: Shared Approaches (CE:SA) a project of Joint Educational Development. To implement the idea, the following committee was appointed representing all four approaches: Mary Duckert, Presbyterian Church (U.S.A), representing Interpreting the Word; Mary Hawkes, United Church of Christ, representing Living the Word and Knowing the Word; Robert Koenig, United Church of Christ, representing Doing the Word; and Cornelia Swain, Cumberland Presbyterian Church, a corresponding member. Paul Hamill, publisher of Gemini Press, was appointed as music consultant. United Church Press accepted responsibility for publishing the Songbook, with Robert Koenig as publisher's representative, and Mary Hawkes and Paul Hamill as editors.

The committee began its work by gathering all the songs and hymns contained in the CE:SA resources. Because there were far too many to be included in a songbook, the following criteria were developed for selecting songs and hymns for inclusion:

- Words and music had to be of acceptable poetic and musical quality.
- The words had to be theologically and educationally sound, and of general educational usefulness.
- Words and music had to be suitable for use with children or young people.
- Inclusive language texts were to be used wherever possible.
- The final list needed to be balanced in its coverage of educational themes for Christian education.

By applying these criteria, approximately one hundred hymns and songs were identified from the CE:SA resources. The rest of the selections were drawn from an examination of other hymnals and songbooks and from suggestions sent in to the committee.

The preparation of a songbook requires much work beyond the selection of hymns and songs. Many hours were spent by the editors checking texts, music, and sources. In some cases, new words, tunes, or harmonies had to be created or found. Special appreciation is due to Jane Graves, Caroline Carroll, and Sandra Ley, who prepared the manuscript and made every effort to track down permissions.

We trust that this songbook will be used with joy and appreciation by many in worship, in the Christian education programs of our churches, and in camps and conferences.

Introduction

Come, let us make a joyful noise to God,
  as we serve with gladness;
Let us come into God's presence with singing,
  as we sing old or new songs;
Let us worship God with voice and dance
  and with sound of instrument;
Let all that breathes sing songs of love
  to our God.

—Paraphrase, Psalms 100, 149, 150

With the Psalmist, we, too, come into God's presence with singing! The Christian church traditionally is a singing church. We are a worshiping church, and through the ages, our peoples have brought music and religion together as they shared their joy and sorrow with their God.

Because the Christian Education: Shared Approaches represent traditions in which music has enhanced the faith, it is appropriate that a collection of songs and hymns be among the resources available. It is appropriate that these songs and hymns be suitable for use with all ages in a variety of settings.

Worship Is First

At the very heart of religious faith is worship. All definitions of religion make reference to the worship of god or gods. In worship, persons have witnessed to the true and the beautiful. Central to the Christian faith is worship in the name of Jesus that contains remembrance of God's goodness, offering of thanks, prayers of love and forgiveness, seeking of God's wisdom and strength for daily living for ourselves and others, and re-commitment toward giving our lives in love and service to God and to our human community and world.

Worship has different meanings for different people; it carries a variety of experiences and emphases at different stages in our lives. Throughout our life span, we may develop new understandings and definitions within our patterns of worship. The development of these understandings is an important aspect of our faith. We are challenged to give our children and youth the highest quality of training in worship—worship in a variety of settings.

Some churches feel that children as part of their development should be present from time to time, or each week, in the corporate worship of the congregation—not only for family worship or for the first ten minutes of the service. A valuable part of the education of children and youth is the understanding that the adult congregation participates in the act of confession or in the offering of themselves as well as in the hymn, call to worship, and children's sermon.

By singing psalms and spiritual songs, the people of God are living up to a long tradition of bringing music and words together to enhance and affect the life of the faith community. The Hebrews expressed their faith through psalms and chants. These formed the bases for worship in the early church, and thus began the practice that we carry on today. On through the forming of the Roman mass, the building of the Gothic cathedral, the spreading of the Protestant Reformation, the proclaiming of the revival message, the struggling of the Black slave, and the challenging of the liberation movement, song and prayer have been united in active expressions of the faith of our people. Hymns and sacred songs have influenced the theological beliefs of our people.

Through music, then, we link ourselves to our rich heritage and to our contemporary world as we share our lives with God in worship. Through experiences with children and youth in our churches, it is important to keep a balance between the music of our heritage and contemporary expression of music. Both aspects are needed as we select songs and hymns for church education.

Selecting Songs and Hymns

Criteria to be considered as we select songs and hymns and introduce them to children, youth, and intergenerational groups include the following:

1. What we use with children when they are very young will influence their taste and understanding in later years, both in terms of music and theology; therefore, we need to give them the very best.

2. Musically, we need to ask if the song or hymn is singable. Often the simplest tunes are the most singable, emphasizing the value of folk music. Is the song within the range of children's voices? As a general rule, young children sing best between middle "C" and the octave above. As children get older, their range may broaden, but for

congregational worship it is best not to go lower than middle "C" or higher than the "E" one octave and two notes above. Is the rhythm simple and not too difficult? Is the harmony pleasing and strong with agreeable chord progressions?

3. Theologically, we must check the words for:
   • Solid biblical understanding;
   • Sound concepts of God, Jesus, and the church;
   • Strong affirmations of our humanity;
   • The inclusive nature of the faith community.

   All of these are true to the integrity of our tradition. We need to be assured of expressions of praise and commitment that reflect sincerely the moods and emphases of the church. Are the concepts understandable to the age range of our group? Are they filled with symbolism and ideas not yet within the understanding of the youngest member of our group?

4. Developmentally, does the song assist children and youth in growing toward a healthy self concept without an overemphasis on the self, so that persons are reaching out to others?

5. Socially, is the language inclusive of all persons, sharing a healthy understanding of the ages, races, and sexes of our society?

6. Educationally, does the song have a message that assists children and youth to grow? Does it speak to the young persons with whom we are working at their age, experience, and capacity levels?

7. Do the participants know the song? If our service of worship is meant to be dignified, it may not lend itself to teaching songs during worship. If it is informal with conversation, learning a song properly may be part of the worship experience.

8. Does the song or hymn lend itself to and enhance our theme for worship?

Teaching Songs and Hymns

Here are a few suggestions for persons who teach songs and hymns to children, youth, and intergenerational groups:

1. As suggested above, it is better not to teach songs during formal services of worship. Use an earlier time even if it's ten minutes before the service begins.

2. If the children are not able to read from song books with small print, use word charts in the front of the room that have large lettering on them. It is helpful to have a teacher sing the words to the songs and point to them, in addition to having an accompanist.

3. To produce good sound, participants should stand erect, keep their books up, and hold their heads high so that they are not swallowing their words but are breathing deeply. Don't emphasize such discipline so strongly, however, that it takes away the enjoyment of singing.

4. If you do not feel comfortable with your own singing abilities, do not be embarrassed. Ask a member of your choir or your church musician to make a tape for use in the classroom.

5. Teach the melody first; then add descants or parts if indicated.

6. While teaching a hymn, it is good to discuss the meaning of the concepts so that children and youth share their understandings.

7. If a hymn or song is used several times, it may be learned and understood with greater satisfaction.

8. Other leaders in the class or department can help by joining the group as it sings.

9. Encourage creativity and originality: Invite participants to make up words, music, and movements to support certain themes or to use with other music or words. Use art work to illustrate the message of a song. Let the children or youth pantomime or paint what the song means to them.

10. We can't all be great musicians, but we can ask:
    • Am I willing to do the best with what I have to teach the meaningful music of the church?
    • Am I open to musical growth in myself and others?
    • Am I listening to children and others to hear the musical sounds they make as they browse, work, or enter a room?
    • Am I sensitive to the dance and movement within persons?

Using Instruments and Movement

Praise God with the timbrel and the dance.
—Psalm 150

Again with the Psalmist, we, too, can praise God with rhythm and movement.

Experiment with the use of instruments to accompany singing. Perhaps there is an instrumentalist in one of your classes who might like to play an obligato. We may know of a person who plays the autoharp or guitar who could be invited to lead the singing from time to time. Such instruments can be used in place of the piano accompaniment. Simple rhythm instruments of good quality lend a spirit of celebration to worship. Instruments can be purchased or made by children or youth. Someone with training and access to Carl Orff instruments might be willing to visit occasionally. The Orff method, named for the contemporary composer, uses percussion instruments in a variety of rhythms, allowing participants opportunity to improvise creatively. Use your own creativity or ingenuity, but be sure of the attitude of the participants—that they bring a celebrative spirit while maintaining a worshipful sense.

The same may be said for movement. For persons of faith, all of life expresses God's presence. Our movements are symbolic and express the wholeness of our beings. Such utterances are a part of our biblical faith. It is important to encourage freedom within children and youth to explore and experiment with movement. Creative movement may be used with even the most traditional hymns. Again use your own creativity and ingenuity.

This is Our CE:SA Songbook

The categories covered in this book are:

Praise and Thanksgiving
God's Love and Care
God's World
Faith and Hope
Worship and Prayer
Jesus: Advent
Jesus: Birth
Jesus: Life and Ministry
Jesus: Resurrection
Christian Tradition
The Church Today
Community
Discipleship and Mission
God's Global Family
Peace and Justice

Each category is preceded by a divider page that includes a descriptive paragraph about the contents and a symbol depicting the concepts.

Language Changes

In order to be inclusive and contemporary in our use of language, we have made a considerable number of changes in the words. Sexist language has been eliminated wherever possible, and words such as "thee," "thou," and "thy," have been modernized. The English language no longer has a commonly used familiar form for "you," as has German with "Du" or French with "tu." For children particularly, we need to use the familiar "you" rather than the unfamiliar "thou." We have omitted the use of terms such as "Lord" or "King" for God, but we have kept them in reference to Jesus, as the first creed of the church stated, "Jesus is Lord."

We have maintained the traditional usage in a few cases, either because we were not given permission to make changes and yet wanted to include the selection, or because we would be violating a tradition or heritage by changing words of a psalm or spiritual. If the group includes persons with handicaps, leaders should use their discretion in the use of songs that may not be inclusive.

Selection of Words and Tunes

There is no rule in hymnology that one particular set of words has to be used with one particular tune. Check your church's hymnbook, for instance, and observe how many sets of words may be used with the same well-known tune.

We sometimes have used familiar tunes with unfamiliar or new words. If children have learned a familiar hymn tune, they will feel at home and be able to sing the hymn when they join the congregation in worship, even though the words they learned might have been difficult. We also have used some new tunes with familiar words—a fresh approach to singing and worshiping together!

JED partner denominations have had opportunity to ask some of their educators and musicians to read the first draft of *Sing to God: Songs and Hymns for Christian Education* and to make suggestions of songs and hymns to be included. We are grateful for their serious and constructive comments and have tried to honor them as we could.

Resources Available

SING TO GOD is available in two editions:

- An edition for leaders, containing all the selections with complete harmonization and appropriate chording. Occasionally comments are given for information or ideas on text, tune, usage, historical background, or use of movement and instruments.
- An edition for children and youth, containing all selections with only the melody line, words and some chording for autoharp or guitar—suitable for use in camps and conferences, and with intergenerational groups, as well as in the classroom.
- In addition, some of the songs and rhythms have been taped for use with children in kindergarten and grades 1 and 2.

Be sure to purchase enough copies of the songbook so that each person has her or his own copy. Songbooks could be given to children as gifts at special times of the year.

Use SING TO GOD in:

- Church school classes.
- Family worship, family nights.
- Intergenerational events.
- Regular Sunday services of worship.
- Departmental worship.
- Homes.
- Choirs.
- Camps and conferences.

Use it anywhere persons might sing—even at parties!

With all these thoughts and hopes, we bring you SING TO GOD: SONGS AND HYMNS FOR CHRISTIAN EDUCATION. We hope that you will sing from it in worship, use it as an educational resource, and enjoy it in your church groups.

We invite you and persons in your church, home, or camp to *Sing to God* in joy and peace!

Mary N. Hawkes

Praise and Thanksgiving

As we sing our alleluias in psalms and hymns of adoration to God, we lift up our voices and gather for worship that enlightens us and allows us to express our joy. We are thankful for the harvest and God's bounty, for families and friends, for health and food, for each new day with its little gifts, and for work. We seek God's will and love, praying for God's promises to be fulfilled and God's light to fill us with fullness.

All Creatures of our God and Light

Psalm 148
Francis of Assisi, 1225
Tr. William Draper
Adapted by Douglas Adams, 1977

LASST UNS ERFREUEN L.M. with Alleluias
Geistliche Kirchengesäng, Cologne, 1623
Harm. by Ralph Vaughan Williams, 1872–1958

1

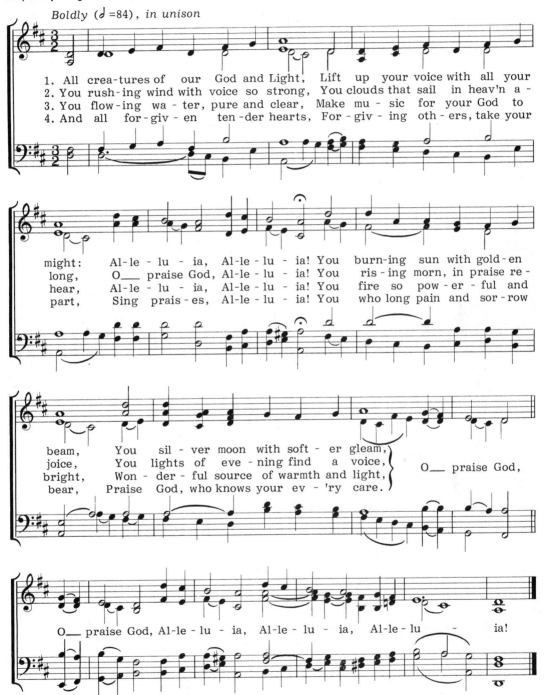

Boldly (♩=84), *in unison*

1. All crea-tures of our God and Light, Lift up your voice with all your might: Al-le-lu-ia, Al-le-lu-ia! You burn-ing sun with gold-en beam, You sil-ver moon with soft-er gleam,
2. You rush-ing wind with voice so strong, You clouds that sail in heav'n a-long, O__ praise God, Al-le-lu-ia! You ris-ing morn, in praise re-joice, You lights of eve-ning find a voice,
3. You flow-ing wa-ter, pure and clear, Make mu-sic for your God to hear, Al-le-lu-ia, Al-le-lu-ia! You fire so pow-er-ful and bright, Won-der-ful source of warmth and light,
4. And all for-giv-en ten-der hearts, For-giv-ing oth-ers, take your part, Sing prais-es, Al-le-lu-ia! You who long pain and sor-row bear, Praise God, who knows your ev-'ry care.

O__ praise God, O__ praise God, Al-le-lu-ia, Al-le-lu-ia, Al-le-lu-ia!

Francis of Assisi, who founded the Order of Franciscans, loved all of creation. He possessed such a gift of joyous song, as found in this hymn, that he was called "God's Troubadour."

2   All the Heavens Your Name Adore

Nestorian Hymn (600–900 A.D.)
Adapted by Mary N. Hawkes, 1983

LIANG CHI-FANG 7.7.7.7.
Nestorian Hymn

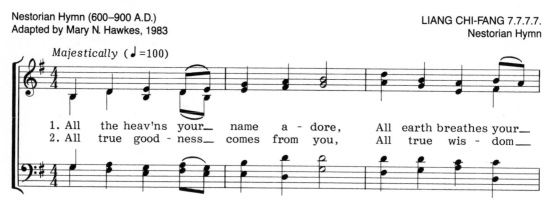

1. All the heav'ns your___ name a - dore, All earth breathes your___
2. All true good - ness___ comes from you, All true wis - dom___

tran - quil peace, All shall glo - ri - fy your power,
sings your praise, All true rev - 'rence ends in you,

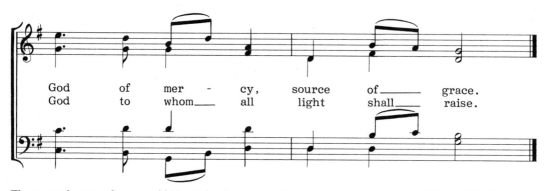

God of mer - cy, source of___ grace.
God to whom___ all light shall___ raise.

These words come from an old Nestorian hymn, dated somewhere between A.D. 600 and 900. Nestorian Christians were found in Persia (today called Iran) and India and introduced Christianity to China. They were a minority people, but they helped to spread Christianity to the East.

Come, Christians, Join to Sing

3

Christian Henry Bateman, 1843
Adapted by Mary N. Hawkes, 1983

MADRID 6.6.6.6.D.
Source Unknown
Harm. by David Evans, 1874–1948

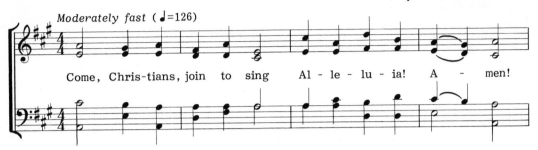

Come, Chris-tians, join to sing Al - le - lu - ia! A - men!

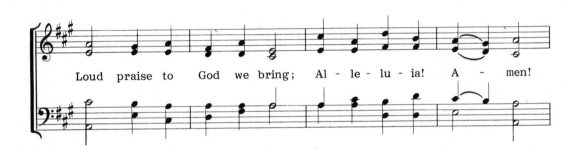

Loud praise to God we bring; Al - le - lu - ia! A - men!

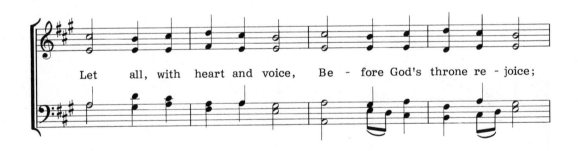

Let all, with heart and voice, Be - fore God's throne re - joice;

Praise we with grate-ful choice: Al - le - lu - ia! A - men!

4

For All the Strength We Have

Maria M. Penstone, 1859–1910

ST. MICHAEL S.M.
Adapted from *Genevan Psalter,* 1551

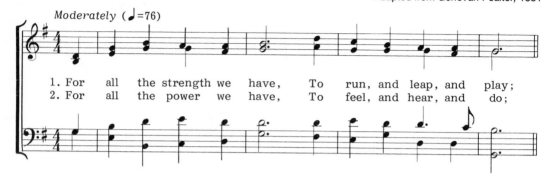

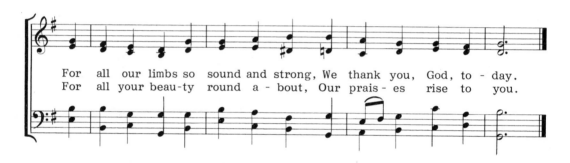

1. For all the strength we have, To run, and leap, and play;
2. For all the power we have, To feel, and hear, and do;

For all our limbs so sound and strong, We thank you, God, to - day.
For all your beau-ty round a - bout, Our prais - es rise to you.

5

I Will Sing Unto God

Psalms 104:33
Altered, 1983

Michael Morgan

I will sing un - to God as long as I

live; I will sing un - to God as long as I live.

Joyful, Joyful, We Adore You

Henry van Dyke, 1902
Words adapted, 1974, 1981, 1983

HYMN TO JOY 8.7.8.7.D.
Arr. from Ludwig van Beethoven, 1770–1827

Moderately fast (♩=126)

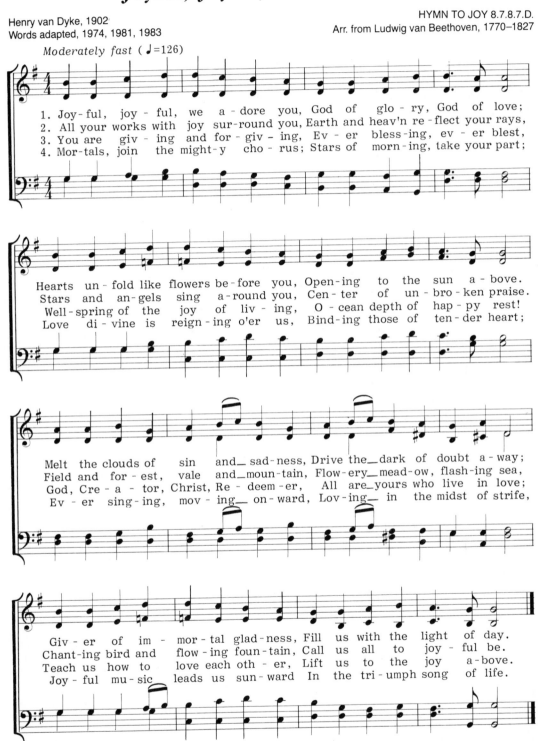

1. Joy-ful, joy-ful, we a-dore you, God of glo-ry, God of love;
2. All your works with joy sur-round you, Earth and heav'n re-flect your rays,
3. You are giv-ing and for-giv-ing, Ev-er bless-ing, ev-er blest,
4. Mor-tals, join the might-y cho-rus; Stars of morn-ing, take your part;

Hearts un-fold like flowers be-fore you, Open-ing to the sun a-bove.
Stars and an-gels sing a-round you, Cen-ter of un-bro-ken praise.
Well-spring of the joy of liv-ing, O-cean depth of hap-py rest!
Love di-vine is reign-ing o'er us, Bind-ing those of ten-der heart;

Melt the clouds of sin and sad-ness, Drive the dark of doubt a-way;
Field and for-est, vale and moun-tain, Flow-ery mead-ow, flash-ing sea,
God, Cre-a-tor, Christ, Re-deem-er, All are yours who live in love;
Ev-er sing-ing, mov-ing on-ward, Lov-ing in the midst of strife,

Giv-er of im-mor-tal glad-ness, Fill us with the light of day.
Chant-ing bird and flow-ing foun-tain, Call us all to joy-ful be.
Teach us how to love each oth-er, Lift us to the joy a-bove.
Joy-ful mu-sic leads us sun-ward In the tri-umph song of life.

"Joyful, Joyful, We Adore You" is adapted from Henry van Dyke with the permission of Charles Scribner's Sons from *The Poems of Henry van Dyke*. Words adapted by the Ecumenical Women's Center, copyright 1975, and further adapted by Grace Moore and Ruth Duck. All sources used by permission.

This tune is the main theme of the choral finale of Beethoven's *Ninth Symphony*. Ralph Vaughan Williams called this theme "one of the greatest melodies of the world." The present hymn arrangement first appeared in *The Hymnal* (Presbyterian), 1911.

7 Now Thank We All Our God

Martin Rinckart, 1586–1649
Tr. Catherine Winkworth, 1827–1878
Altered, 1983

NUN DANKET 6.7.6.7.6.6.6.6.
Melody by Johann Crüger, 1648
Adapted by Felix Mendelssohn, 1840

Majestically (♩=84), *in unison*

1. Now thank we all our God With heart and hands and voic - es,
2. O may this boun-teous God Through all our life be near us,

Who won-drous things has done, In whom God's world re - joic - es,
With ev - er joy - ful hearts And bless - ed peace to cheer us,

Who, from our moth - ers' arms, Has blessed us on our way
And keep us filled with grace, And guide us when per - plexed,

With count-less gifts of love, And still is ours to - day.
And free us from all ills In this world and the next.

This tune first appeared with the "Nun danket" text in 1648. Johann Crüger is known for his beautiful chorale melodies. During his forty years as cantor of the Church of St. Nicolai, Crüger became the leading musical figure in Berlin.

Praise God for Our Blessings All

8

Nancy Livingston Goff

Nancy Livingston Goff

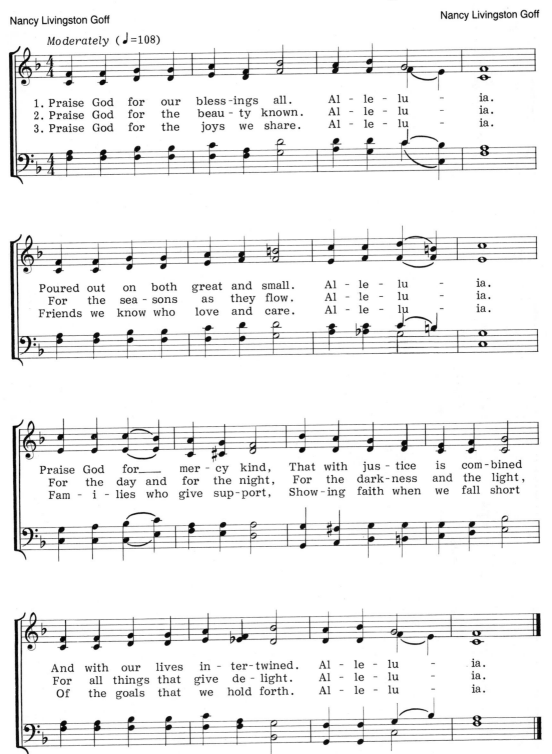

Moderately (♩=108)

1. Praise God for our bless-ings all. Al - le - lu - ia.
2. Praise God for the beau - ty known. Al - le - lu - ia.
3. Praise God for the joys we share. Al - le - lu - ia.

Poured out on both great and small. Al - le - lu - ia.
For the sea - sons as they flow. Al - le - lu - ia.
Friends we know who love and care. Al - le - lu - ia.

Praise God for mer - cy kind, That with jus - tice is com - bined
For the day and for the night, For the dark - ness and the light,
Fam - i - lies who give sup-port, Show - ing faith when we fall short

And with our lives in - ter-twined. Al - le - lu - ia.
For all things that give de - light. Al - le - lu - ia.
Of the goals that we hold forth. Al - le - lu - ia.

9

Our Thanks to You, O God

Lyn Beckwith, 1963
Altered, 1983

TALLIS' CANON L.M.
Thomas Tallis, c. 1567

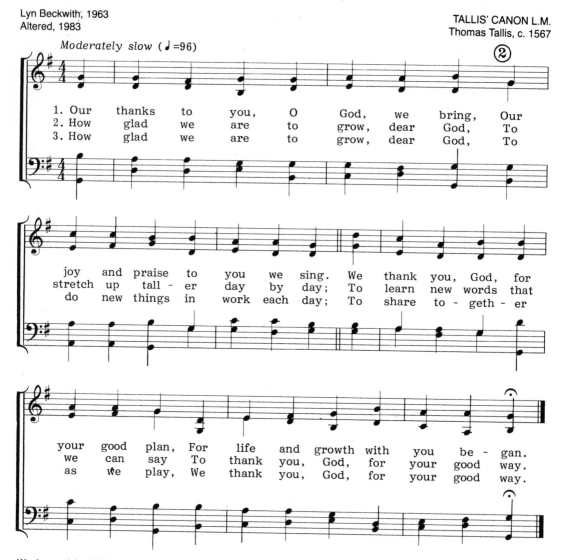

1. Our thanks to you, O God, we bring, Our joy and praise to you we sing. We thank you, God, for your good plan, For life and growth with you be - gan.
2. How glad we are to grow, dear God, To stretch up tall - er day by day; To learn new words that we can say To thank you, God, for your good way.
3. How glad we are to grow, dear God, To do new things in work each day; To share to - geth - er as we play, We thank you, God, for your good way.

This arrangement of the Tallis tune dates from Ravenscroft's *Whole Booke of Psalmes,* 1621. *The Harvard Dictionary of Music* defines a canon as a "polyphonic composition in which all the parts have the same melody throughout, although starting at different points." To sing this as a canon, divide the singers into two groups. Have the first group sing unaccompanied. The second group enters when the first group reaches (2). Children might enjoy adding new verses to this old tune.(Apel, Willi. *Harvard Dictionary of Music.* Cambridge, Harvard Univ. Press, 1950, page 112).

10 ## Praise and Thanksgiving Let Everyone Bring

Traditional
Paraphrase of the German
Altered, 1983

LOBET UND PREISET Irr.
Alsatian Round

With movement (♩ = 108)

Praise and thanks - giv - ing let ev - 'ry one bring
Lob - et und preis - et ihr Völk - er den Herrn;

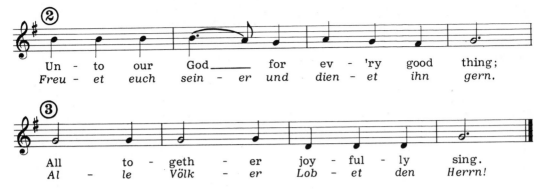

Un - to our God_____ for ev - 'ry good thing;
Freu - et euch sein - er und dien - et ihn gern.

All to - geth - er joy - ful - ly sing.
Al - le Völk - er Lob - et den Herrn!

From The *Whole World Singing* compiled by Edith Lovell Thomas, Friendship Press, 1950. Used by permission.

May be sung as a three-part round.

Praise to God With Adoration

11

From Psalms 149, 150
M. H. Beck, 1975
Adapted, 1983

SHIPSTON 8.7.8.7.
English Melody
Harm. by Paul Hamill, 1983

Rhythmically (♩=108)

1. Praise to God with ad - o - ra - tion!
2. Shake the tam - bou - rine_____ and_____ shak - ers,
3. Sing out loud and skip_____ in_____ danc - es!

You are good and you___ are___ strong. You have_ shown the
Ring the bells and beat_ the_ drum! We will_ have a
You are great and yours_ we_ are. Clap our_ hands and

world you love us. So we praise you___ in our song.
cel - e - bra - tion; Tell the peo - ple___ all to come.
shout your prais - es! You have pow - er___ near and far.

Adapted from the resource packet to *God Loves All People* © 1975 by John Knox Press and used by permission.

The words to this song would make it appropriate for using instruments.

12 Praise, O Praise Our God, O Sing

Psalm 136, based on John Milton's Version, 1623
Rev. Henry Williams Baker (1821–1877)
Altered 1979, 1983

INNOCENTS 7.7.7.7.
The Parish Choir, 1850
W. H. Monk, 1823–1889

1. Praise, O praise our God, O sing
2. Praise our God who made the sun
3. Praise our God who gave the rain
4. God did bid the fruit - ful field
5. To our boun - teous God, O sing

Hymns of ad - o - ra - tion sing; For God's mer - cies
Day by day its course to run; For God's mer - cies
To ma - ture the swell - ing grain; For God's mer - cies
Crops of pre - cious in - crease yield; For God's mer - cies
Glo - ry let cre - a - tion sing, Glo - ry to the

still en - dure, Ev - er faith - ful, ev - er sure.
still en - dure, Ev - er faith - ful, ev - er sure.
still en - dure, Ev - er faith - ful, ev - er sure.
still en - dure, Ev - er faith - ful, ev - er sure.
Ma - ker, Son, And blest Spir - it, Three in One!

This tune is associated with the Oxford Movement and has often been attributed to George Frederick Handel. Erik Routley assigns this tune to William H. Monk, music editor of *Hymns Ancient and Modern,* 1861.

Praise Our God, O Praise Be Given

13

Author Unknown
Adapted by Mary N. Hawkes, 1983

PRAISE OUR GOD 8.7.8.7.D.
Frederick Parsonage

Joyfully (♩=112), in unison

1. Praise our God, O Praise be giv - en Un - to God our great de - light. Sun and moon by God are ris - en; Praise God through all stars and light. Praise, O praise, for God has spo - ken; Worlds God's might - y voice o - beyed: Laws which nev - er shall be bro - ken, For our guid - ance God has made.

2. Praise our God, whose Love is glo - ri - ous; Nev - er shall God's prom - ise fail: God has made all saints vic - to - ri - ous; Sin and death shall not pre - vail. Praise the God of our sal - va - tion; Hosts on high God's power pro - claim; Heaven and earth and all cre - a - tion, Laud and mag - ni - fy God's name!

14 Rock of Ages, Let Our Song

Leopold Stein
Tr. M. Jastrow and G. Gottheil
Adapted by Mary N. Hawkes, 1983

ROCK OF AGES 7.6.7.6.6.6.6.6.
Hebrew Melody

Majestically (♩=92)

1. Rock of A - ges, let our song Praise God's sav - ing pow - er;
2. Kin - dling new the ho - ly lamps, Priests ap - proved in suf - fer - ing,
3. Chil - dren of the mar - tyr race, Wheth - er free or fet - tered,

God a - midst the rag - ing foes, Was our shel - t'ring tow - er.
Pu - ri - fied the na - tion's shrine, Brought to God their of - fer - ing.
Wake the ech - oes of the songs Where you may be scat - tered!

Fu - rious they bom - bard - ed, God's own arm it guard - ed,
And God's courts sur - round - ing Hear, in joy a - bound - ing,
Yours the mes - sage cheer - ing, That the time is near - ing

And God's word broke their sword, When our own strength failed us.
Hap - py throngs sing - ing songs Far and wide re - sound - ing.
When all per - sons are free Ty - rants dis - ap - pear - ing.

This Hebrew hymn expresses praise and joy in God who is our strength. It may be sung to commemorate Hanukkah, the Jewish festival of lights, honoring the rededication of the temple at Jerusalem in 165 B.C. under Judas Maccabeus.

The God of Abraham Praise

15

Revised Version of the *Yigdal*
Daniel ben Judah c. 1400
Tr. Newton Mann, 1836–1926 and
Max Landsberg, 1845–1928, adapted 1983

LEONI 6.6.8.4.D.
Hebrew Melody
Adapted by Meyer Lyno, 1770

1. The God of A-braham praise, All prais-ed be God's name.
2. God's spir-it flow-eth free, High surg-ing where it will:
3. God has e-ter-nal life Im-plant-ed in the soul:

Who was and is, and is to be, For aye the same!
In proph-et's word God spoke of old And calls us still.
God's love shall be our strength and stay, While a-ges roll.

The one e-ter-nal God, Ere_ aught_ that_ now ap-pears:
Es-tab-lished is God's law, And_ change-less_ it shall stand.
Praise to the liv-ing God! All_ prais-ed_ be God's name.

The First, the Last; be-yond all_thought through time-less years!
Deep writ up-on the hu-man_ heart, On____ sea, or land.
Who was, and is, and is to_ be, For____ aye the same!

These words are from the *Yigdal,* the Hebrew doxology based on the thirteen articles of the Jewish creed.
There are seven melodies associated with the *Yigdal.*

Thank You, Thank You

Richard Avery

Donald Marsh

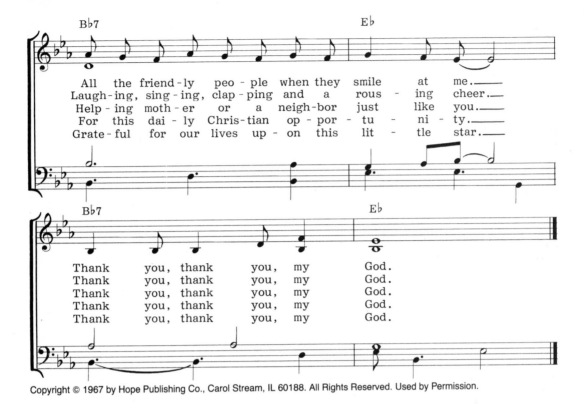

All the friend-ly peo-ple when they smile at me.
Laugh-ing, sing-ing, clap-ping and a rous-ing cheer.
Help-ing moth-er or a neigh-bor just like you.
For this dai-ly Chris-tian op-por-tu-ni-ty.
Grate-ful for our lives up-on this lit-tle star.

Thank you, thank you, my God.
Thank you, thank you, my God.
Thank you, thank you, my God.
Thank you, thank you, my God.
Thank you, thank you, my God.

This is the Day That Our God Has Made 17

Anonymous
Altered, 1983

THIS IS THE DAY Irr.
Fiji Islands Folk Melody

Brightly (♩ = 126)

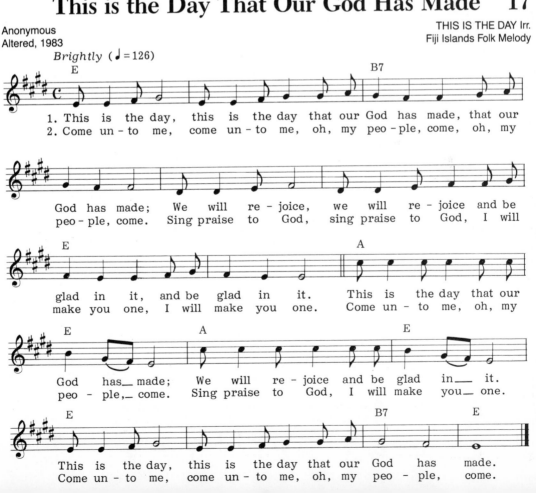

1. This is the day, this is the day that our God has made, that our
2. Come un-to me, come un-to me, oh, my peo-ple, come, oh, my

God has made; We will re-joice, we will re-joice and be
peo-ple, come. Sing praise to God, sing praise to God, I will

glad in it, and be glad in it. This is the day that our
make you one, I will make you one. Come un-to me, oh, my

God has_ made; We will re-joice and be glad in_ it.
peo-ple,_ come. Sing praise to God, I will make you_ one.

This is the day, this is the day that our God has made.
Come un-to me, come un-to me, oh, my peo-ple, come.

18   Serve Our God With Joy and Gladness

Based on Psalms 11:2
Mary E. Huey, 1959

CHARLESTOWN 8.7.8.7.
Sacred Harmony, No. 1, 1803
Harm. by Paul Hamill, 1983

Moderately (♩=88), *in unison*

Serve our God with_ joy and glad-ness; Come in -
to God's gates with song; Serve our_ God with
lov - ing kind-ness; Love and praise God all day long.

Words copyright, 1963, by W. L. Jenkins; from *Songs and Hymns for Primary Children.* Used by permission of The Westminster Press.

19   To God Who Gives Us Daily Bread

Attr. to Mary Rumsey
Altered, 1983

TALLIS' ORDINAL
Thomas Tallis, c. 1567

Moderately (♩=112)

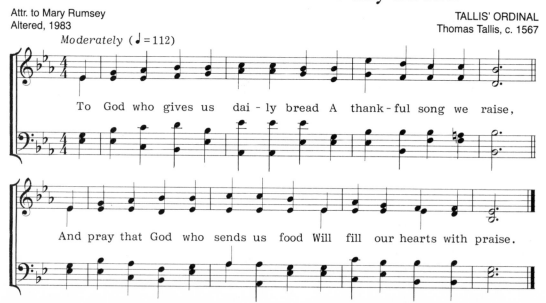

To God who gives us dai - ly bread A thank - ful song we raise,
And pray that God who sends us food Will fill our hearts with praise.

Jean S. Parkinson

ST. FLAVIAN C.M.
Adapted from *Day's Psalter*, 1562

Moderately (♩=76), *in unison*

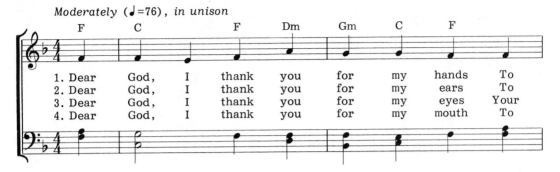

1. Dear God, I thank you for my hands To
2. Dear God, I thank you for my ears To
3. Dear God, I thank you for my eyes Your
4. Dear God, I thank you for my mouth To

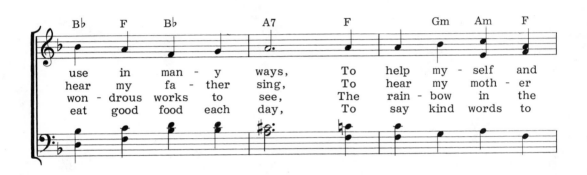

use in man - y ways, To help my - self and
hear my fa - ther sing, To hear my moth - er
won - drous works to see, The rain - bow in the
eat good food each day, To say kind words to

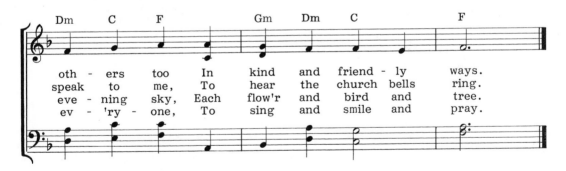

oth - ers too In kind and friend - ly ways.
speak to me, To hear the church bells ring.
eve - ning sky, Each flow'r and bird and tree.
ev - 'ry - one, To sing and smile and pray.

This song should be used carefully, as some persons in the group may have handicaps. The text may be used in these cases as a teaching tool.

God's Love and Care

Wherever we go and whatever we do, God's faithfulness and love surround us. Because of God's gift of life and growth, we mature from childhood through adulthood; we find our rest in God, knowing that our prayers always are heard.

How Strong and Kind Is God's Good Care 21

Source Unknown
Altered, 1983

O JESULEIN SÜSS 8.8.8.8.8.8.
Cologne Melody, 1623
Harm. By Johann Sebastian Bach, 1658–1750

Not too fast (♩=96)

How strong___ and kind is God's___ good care That round a - bout me, like___ the air; Is with me al - ways, ev - 'ry - where, Is with me al - ways ev - 'ry - where, How strong___ and kind is God's___ good care.

22 A Star Is Shining at Nighttime

Margaret C. McNeil

Margaret C. McNeil
Harm. by M.E.H.

1. A star is shin-ing at night - time; Night-time's here._
2. The moon is shin-ing at night - time; Night-time's here._

God is al - ways with me. God is here._

Adapted from "Night and Day" in *Come Sing with Me.* Used by permission of The Judson Press.

23 Jesus Said to All the People

Ann Evans

GOD LOVES ME 8.7.7.7.7.7.
Swedish Folk Tune

1. Je-sus said to all the peo-ple As they crowd-ed close to hear,
2. Je-sus said to all the peo-ple As he taught them how to pray,

"God_ loves you as I love you; God is with you ev - 'ry-where."
"God_ loves you as I love you; God_ knows the prayers you pray."

Je-sus showed that God_ loves me, God is with me ev - 'ry - where.
Je-sus taught that God_ loves me, God_ knows the prayers I pray.

"God Loves Me" by Ann Evans. Music arrangement copyright © 1972 by Graded Press. Used by permission.

Every Morning Seems to Say

24

Henry van Dyke

Grace Wilbur Conant

Brightly (♩=116), in unison

Ev - 'ry morn - ing seems to say, "There's some - thing hap - py on the way, And God sends love to you!"

Henry van Dyke, "Every Morning Seems to Say," in *The House of Rimmon.* Copyright 1908 Charles Scribner's Sons; copyright renewed 1936 Tertius van Dyke. Reprinted with the permission of Charles Scribner's Sons.

Good Morning, God

25

A Church School Class

Norman and Margaret Mealy

Brightly (♪=120), in unison

Good morn - ing, God. Now it is light.

Thank you for sleep and for rest through the night.

From *Come Sing with Me,* copyright by Judson Press. Used by permission of Judson Press.

26   Let Us With a Gladsome Mind

Psalm 136
John Milton, 1623
Adapted, 1983

MONKLAND 7.7.7.7.
John Antes (1740–1811)
Arr. by John Wilkes, 1861

1. Let us with a glad-some mind Praise our God who is so kind:
2. All the liv-ing God doth feed; With full hand sup-plies their need:
3. Let us then with glad-some mind Praise our God who is so kind:

Refrain

For God's mer-cies shall en-dure, Ev-er faith-ful, ev-er sure.

This song could be used antiphonally in worship, with a small group singing the verse and the whole group doing the refrain. The tune is from *Hymn Tunes of the United Brethren,* 1824, a collection in which most of the melodies were taken from German chorales.

27   Our God Is Ever Near

Source Unknown
Altered, 1979

ST. MICHAEL S.M.
Melody by Louis Bourgeois, 1551
Adapted by William Crotch, 1836

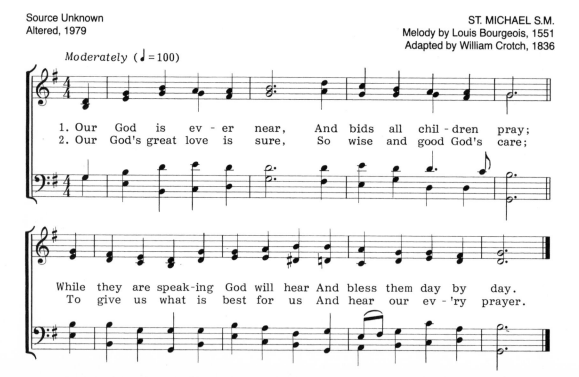

1. Our God is ev-er near, And bids all chil-dren pray;
2. Our God's great love is sure, So wise and good God's care;

While they are speak-ing God will hear And bless them day by day.
To give us what is best for us And hear our ev-'ry prayer.

God Is So Good

Arr. by Sylvester A. Fields

AFRICAN SONG
Arr. by Sylvester A. Fields

Moderately (♩ =88), *in unison*

1. God is so good, God is so good,
2. God cares for me, God cares for me,
3. God loves me so, God loves me so,

God is so good. Yes, God's good to me.
God cares for me. Yes, God cares for me.
God loves me so. Yes, God loves me so.

29 If Anybody Asks You Who I Am

Spiritual from Georgia

THE LITTLE CRADLE ROCKS TONIGHT Irr.
Spiritual from Georgia

Brightly (♩=126), in unison

1. If an-y-bod-y asks you who I am,____ who I am,____ who I am,____ If an-y-bod-y asks you who I am,____ Say that I'm a child of God.____

2. The lit-tle cra-dle rocks to - night in glo - ry, rocks in glo - ry, rocks in glo-ry, The lit-tle cra-dle rocks to - night in glo - ry, Je - sus was born in glo - ry.____

In the first stanza, the words are expressing an assurance of God's love. In the second stanza, the words express the assurance that, as Jesus was born in glory, so are all children.

The Lone, Wild Bird in Lofty Flight   30

Henry Richard McFadyen, 1925
Altered, 1968, 1983

PROSPECT Irr.
Southern Harmony, 1835
Harm. by Paul Hamill, 1983

Slowly (♩=84), *in unison*

1. The lone, wild bird in loft - y flight
2. The ends of earth are in your hand,

Is still with you nor leaves your sight,
The sea's dark deep and far - off land.

And I am yours! I rest in you.

Great Spir - it, come, and rest in me.

Harmony copyright © 1983 The Pilgrim Press.

This tune first appeared in the *Southern Harmony,* 1835.

31   We Grow in Many Different Ways

Dosia Carlson, 1965, 1983

PISGAH C.M.
Kentucky Harmony, 1817
Attr. to J. C. Lowry

Joyously (♩=104)

1. We grow in man - y____ dif - ferent ways____ Ac -
2. From help - less days____ of____ ba - by hood____ We've____
3. Our bod - ies change____ in____ shape and size;____ Our____
4. Your gifts of life____ and____ growth, O God,____ Help____

cord - ing to____ God's____ plan. A____ girl grows in - to____
grown in height____ and____ weight. And____ ev - 'ry year when____
minds can think____ and____ dream. Our____ eyes and ears, our____
us to un - der - stand That____ praise be - longs to____

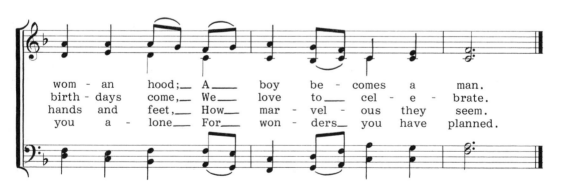

wom - an hood;____ A____ boy be - comes a man.
birth - days come,____ We____ love to____ cel - e - brate.
hands and feet,____ How____ mar - vel - ous they seem.
you a - lone For____ won - ders____ you have planned.

Words used by permission of the author.

We Thank You, God, for Eyes to See

Jeanette Perkins Brown, 1887–1960

FOREST GREEN C.M.D.
English Melody
Arr. by Ralph Vaughan Williams, 1872–1958

In moderate time (♩=96)

We thank you, God, for eyes to see The beau-ty of the earth;

For ears to hear the word of love And hap-py sounds of mirth;

For minds that find new thoughts to think, New won-ders to ex-plore;

For health and free-dom to en-joy The good you have in store.

In working with some groups, interpretation or substitution of some words may be needed, due to the presence of handicapped persons. We may "see" and "hear" symbolically if not physically. This English folk melody was introduced by Ralph Vaughan Williams in *The English Hymnal,* 1906, and was set to the words "O Little Town of Bethlehem."

33 Wherever I May Wander

Ann B. Snow, 1959
Altered, 1979, 1983

New England Folk Tune
Harm. by Irving Lowens, 1955

Not too fast (♩ =76), *in unison*

1. Wher - ev - er I may wan-der, Wher-ev - er I may be, I'm
2. Through-out God's whole cre - a - tion I see such lov-ing care; For

cer - tain of my Mak-er's love; God's care is o - ver me. God
ev - 'ry one in ev - 'ry land, God's chil-dren ev-'ry-where. Wher-

made the great high moun - tains, God made the wide blue sea. God
ev - er I may wan - der, Wher-ev - er I may be. I'm

made the sky, where air-planes fly; God made the world and me.
cer - tain of my Mak-er's love; God's care is o - ver me.

God's World

In the beauty and wisdom of God's natural world, we find joy and feel a sense of wonder. God expresses love to us in the birds, flowers, seeds, butterflies, and bees, and in the steadiness and order in the universe—sun, moon, and stars. We see God's re-creation in this natural world and are thankful, as we promise to live responsibly in caring for the earth.

34　All Things Bright and Beautiful

Cecil F. Alexander, 1818–1895
Altered, 1983

ROYAL OAK 7.6.7.6 with Refrain
English Melody
Adapted by Martin Shaw, 1875–1958

Cheerfully (♩=112), *in unison*

Refrain

All things bright and beau-ti-ful, All crea-tures great and_ small,

All things wise and won-der-ful, Our dear God made them_ all. *Fine*

1. Each lit - tle flower that_ o - pens, Each lit - tle bird_ that sings,
2. The pur - ple - head - ed_ moun-tain, The riv - er run - ning by,
3. The cold wind in the_ win - ter, The pleas-ant sum - mer sun,

Repeat Refrain

God_ made their glow-ing_ col - ors, and_ made their ti - ny_ wings.
The_ sun - set, and the_ morn - ing That_ bright-ens up the_ sky.
The_ ripe fruits in the_ gar - den, God_ made them ev - 'ry_ one.

How Beautiful Is the Green Earth

Frances E. Jacobs, 1931

German Folk Song

How beau-ti-ful is the green earth,_____ The stars in the heav-en a-bove!_____ But what would the whole world be worth If we did not fill it with Love, with Love, If we did not fill it with Love?_____

36 How Wonderful This World of God's

F. Pratt Green
Adapted by Mary N. Hawkes, 1983

ALLGÜTIGER, MEIN PREISGESANG 8.8.6.D.
Georg Peter Weimer, 1734–1800

Majestically (♩=104)

1. How won-der-ful this world__ of__ God's,
2. The small-est seed in se-cret__ grows,
3. The mi-grant bird, in win-ter__ fled,
4. O God, whose great-er gifts__ are__ ours:

A frag-ment of a fi-er-y sun, How love-ly__ and how
And thrust-ing up-ward an-swers soon The bid-ding__ of the
Shall come a-gain with spring and build In this same__ sha-dy
A con-scious will, a think-ing mind, A heart that's__ wor-ship-

small! Where all things serve God's__ great de-sign, Where
light; The bud un-furls in-to a rose; The
tree; By se-cret wis-dom__ sure-ly led, Home-
ful. O take these strange un-fold-ing powers And

life's ad-ven-ture__ is be-gun In God, the__ life of all.
wings with-in the__ white co-coon Are per-fect-ed for flight.
ward a-cross the__ clo-ver-field Hur-ries the__ hon-ey-bee.
teach us through your__ Son to find The life more__ free and full.

I Sing the Mighty Power of God

37

Issac Watts, 1674–1748
Adapted by Mary N. Hawkes, 1983

ELLACOMBE C.M.D.
Gesangbuch, Wirtemberg, 1784

Moderately fast (♩=116)

1. I sing the mighty power of God, That made the mountains rise,
2. I sing the goodness of the One, Who filled the earth with food;
3. There's not a plant or flower below, But makes your glories known.

That spread the flowing seas abroad, And built the lofty skies.
Who formed the creatures with a word, And then pronounced them good.
And clouds arise, and tempests blow, By order from your throne.

I sing the wisdom that ordained The sun to rule the day,
God, how your wonders are displayed, Wher-e'er I turn my eye:
While all that from you borrows life Is ever in your care,

The moon shines full at God's command, And all the stars obey.
If I survey the ground I tread, Or gaze upon the sky!
And even where there's grief and strife, Your love is always there.

38

Many and Great, O God

Based on Jeremiah 10:6–13
Dakota Indian Hymnal
Paraphrase by F. Philip Frazier, 1892–1964
Altered, 1983

LAQUIPARLE Irr.
Sioux Indian Melody

Slowly (♩ =100), *in unison*

1. Man - y and great, O God, are your things, Mak - er of
2. Grant un - to us com - mun - ion with you, O star - a -

earth and sky; Your hands have set the heav - ens with stars;
bid - ing One; Come un - to us and dwell with___ us,

Your fin - gers spread the moun - tains and plains. Lo, at your
With you are found the gifts of___ life. Bless us with

word the wa - ters were formed; Deep seas o - bey your voice.
life that has no___ end, E - ter - nal life with you.

The Dakota Indian Hymnal was compiled in 1879 by Rev. Thomas Williamson and Rev. Stephen Return Riggs, Presbyterian and Congregational missionaries to the Dakota Indians. The words to this song reflect an understanding of Jeremiah. F. Philip Frazier, who paraphrased the words, was a grandson of Artemas Ehnamani, the first ordained minister of the Dakota tribe. Frazier, too, was an ordained minister, and he and his wife were fine singers who gave concerts to raise money for their work among the Indians.

Morning Has Broken

Eleanor Farjeon, 1881–1965

BUNESSAN 5.5.5.4.D.
Gaelic Melody
Harm. by Paul Hamill, 1984

Moderately (♩=96), in unison

1. Morn-ing has bro - ken Like the first morn - ing, Black-bird has spo - ken Like the first bird. ___ Praise for the sing - ing! Praise for the morn - ing! Praise for them, spring - ing Fresh from the Word! ___

2. Mine is the sun - light! Mine is the morn - ing Born of the one light E - den saw play! ___ Praise with e - la - tion, Praise ev - 'ry morn - ing, God's re - cre - a - tion Of the new day! ___

The words were written by Eleanor Farjeon for the tune "Bunessan" at the request of Percy Dearmer, editor of *Songs of Praise*. The melody was first published in 1888. This hymn gained much secular popularity in the 1970s and was recorded by several major recording studios.

40 O God of Stars and Sunlight

John Holmes, 1904–1962
Altered 1983

ES FLOG EIN KLEINS WALDVÖGELEIN 7.6.7.6.D.
Memingen MS., 17th century
Harm. by George Woodward, 1904

Moderately (♩=112)

1. O God of stars and sun - light, Whose wind lifts up a bird,
2. O God of cloud and moun - tain, Whose rain on rock is art,

In march-ing wave and leaf - fall We hear your pa - tient word.
Your plan and care and mean - ing Re - new the head and heart.

The col - or of___your sea - sons Goes gold a - cross the land.
Your word and col - or spo - ken, Your sum -mer noons and showers

By green up - on the tree - tops We know your mov - ing hand.
By these and by your sun - shine, We know your world is ours.

O How Glorious, Full of Wonder

41

Psalm 8
Curtis Beach, 1914-
Adapted, 1983

DEER RUN 8.7.8.7.D.
Paul Hamill, 1983

Brightly (♩=112), in unison

1. O how glo - rious, full of won - der___ Is your name o'er
all the earth; You who wrought cre - a - tion's splen - dor,___
Bring-ing suns and stars to birth! Rapt in rev-erence
we a - dore you, Mar - veling at your mys-tic ways. Hum-bly now we___
bow be - fore you,___ Lift - ing up our hearts in praise.

2. You have giv - en___ us do - min - ion___ O'er the won - ders
of your hand, Made us fly with___ ea - gle pin - ion,___
Guard-ing o - ver sea and land. Soar - ing spire and
ru - ined cit - y; These our hopes and fail-ures show. Teach us more of___
hu - man pit - y,___ That we in your im - age grow.

3. O how won - drous, O how glo - rious___ Is your name in
ev - 'ry land! God, whose pur - pose___ moves be - fore us___
Toward the goal that you have planned. 'Tis your will our
hearts are seek-ing, Con - scious of our hu - man need. Spir - it in our___
spir - it speak - ing,___ Make us wor - ship you in - deed!

The tune "Deer Run" is one of the new hymn tunes especially written for SING TO GOD. Paul Hamill, music editor of SING TO GOD, composer, teacher, and organist, has served Methodist, Episcopal, Presbyterian, and United Church of Christ congregations.

42 Sing a Song of Gladness

Ermine Cross (adapted)
Adapted by Mary N. Hawkes, 1983

Hans Georg Nägeli, 1773–1836

Moderately (♩.=76), in unison

Sing a song of glad - ness! Ev - 'ry-bod - y, sing and sing

1. For
2. For
3. For

Fine

fruits and flow - ers and rain - bows, And ev - 'ry pleas - ant thing.
rob - ins and for blue - birds, And ev - 'ry love - ly thing.
rest - ful nights and sun - ny days, And ev - 'ry good thing.

Move to the music, or sing "la, la," after 2nd stanza

D.C.

The rhythm and free-flowing nature of this song and the interlude make it appropriate for creative move-ment or for using instrumental accompaniment with young children.

The Earth Is Full of Riches

43

Lois Horton Young

LLANFYLLIN 7.6.7.6.D.
Welsh Melody

With spirit (♩ =116)

1. The earth is full of rich - es Planned by God's ten - der care And
2. The grow-ing plants and sys - tems Of life, of law, of space God
3. So on - ly as good stew - ards Have we the right to live And

moved in - to cre - a - tion All or - der - ly and fair. The
spread in boun - ty round ___ us With beau - ty ev - 'ry place. For
bor - row from earth's treas - ures To share, to use, to give. We

springs and streams and o - ceans, Pure-flow-ing, clear, and free, The
all our good and pleas - ure Were all these rich - es planned, But
praise the Great Cre - a - tor For each good gift of worth: For

earth with hid - den treas - ures, God caused all these to be.
not to waste or poi - son With care - less heart or hand.
these days and for fu - ture time We'll cher - ish all God's earth.

Words used by permission of Carl E. Young. Copyright 1984 by United Church Press.

This hymn may be used to teach the good stewardship of the earth. Although God has planned an orderly and beautiful earth, it is up to us to care for it.

Faith and Hope

Our faith is apparent to us in the prophets, in creation, and in Jesus as we observe God's presence in the great dreams and visions of persons of faith. Throughout illness, fear, hardship, struggle, we trust God who is always there. In spite of pain, we may laugh and hope, as we find strength in God's steadfastness and promise of eternal life.

God of Grace and God of Glory

44

Harry Emerson Fosdick, 1930
Adapted, 1983

CWM RHONDDA 8.7.8.7.8.7.7.
John Hughes, 1873–1932

Majestically (♩ =88)

1. God of grace and God of glory, On your people pour your power;
2. Lo! the hosts of e - vil round us Scorn your Christ, as - sail his ways!
3. Cure your chil-dren's war - ring mad-ness; Bend our pride to your con - trol;
4. Save us from weak res - ig - na - tion To the e - vils we de - plore;

Crown your an - cient church's sto - ry; Bring its bud to glo-rious flower.
From the fears that long have bound us, Free our hearts to faith and praise.
Shame our wan - ton, self - ish glad-ness, Rich in things and poor in soul.
Let the search for your sal - va - tion Be our glo - ry ev - er - more.

Grant us wis - dom, Grant us cour - age, For the fac - ing of this
Grant us wis - dom, Grant us cour - age, For the liv - ing of these
Grant us wis - dom, Grant us cour - age, Lest we miss your king-dom's
Grant us wis - dom, Grant us cour - age, Serv - ing you whom we a -

hour, For the fac - ing of this hour.
days, For the liv - ing of these days.
goal, Lest we miss your king - dom's goal.
dore, Serv - ing you whom we a - dore.

45 Grant Us True Courage, God

Stanza 1, Henry W. Foote, 1875–1964
Stanzas 2, 3, Lindell Sawyers, 1982
(Based on Philippians)
Altered, 1983

O GOTT, DU FROMMER GOTT 6.7.6.7.6.6.6.6.
Melody by Ahasuerus Fritsch, 1649–1701
Harm. by J. S. Bach, 1685–1750

Moderately slow (♩=92)

1. Grant us true courage, God, To face each new endeavor;
2. Grant us true vision, God, To see where you are leading;
3. Grant us true wisdom, God, To weigh and choose the better;

Re - ly - ing on your word That you will leave us never;
Re - spond - ing to your word, Your call to service heeding;
Dis - cern - ing in your word The spirit, not the letter;

A - like in gloom or joy Each duty to fulfill,
And where op - pres - sions kill, Your children cry and bend,
The mind of Christ be - stow— His self expending way —

Our minds and hearts employ To do your perfect will.
Our eyes with pity fill, Our hands in love extend.
Un - til at last we know Your kingdom's glorious day.

Stanzas 2 and 3 were written for use at the installation of officers, National Cruise, Presbyterian Mariners, Stanford University, 1982. Lindell Sawyers, Associate for Adult Leader Education and Family Ministries, Presbyterian Church (U.S.A.), is advisor to this group.

If You Will Only Let God Guide You 46

Georg Neumark, 1657
Tr. by Catherine Winkworth, 1827–1878
Altered, 1972

NEUMARK 9.8.9.8.8.8.
Melody by Georg Neumark, 1657

Moderately (♩ = 96)

If you will on - ly let God guide you, And hope in God through

all your ways, What - ev - er comes, God stands be - side you

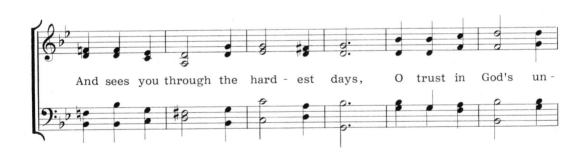

And sees you through the hard - est days, O trust in God's un -

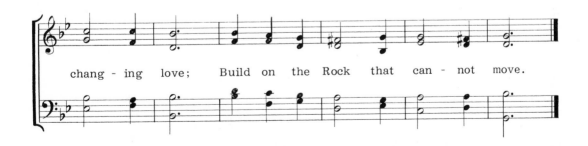

chang - ing love; Build on the Rock that can - not move.

47 I'm Just a Poor Wayfaring Stranger

Traditional

WAYFARING STRANGER Irr.
White Spiritual
Harm. by Paul Hamill, 1983

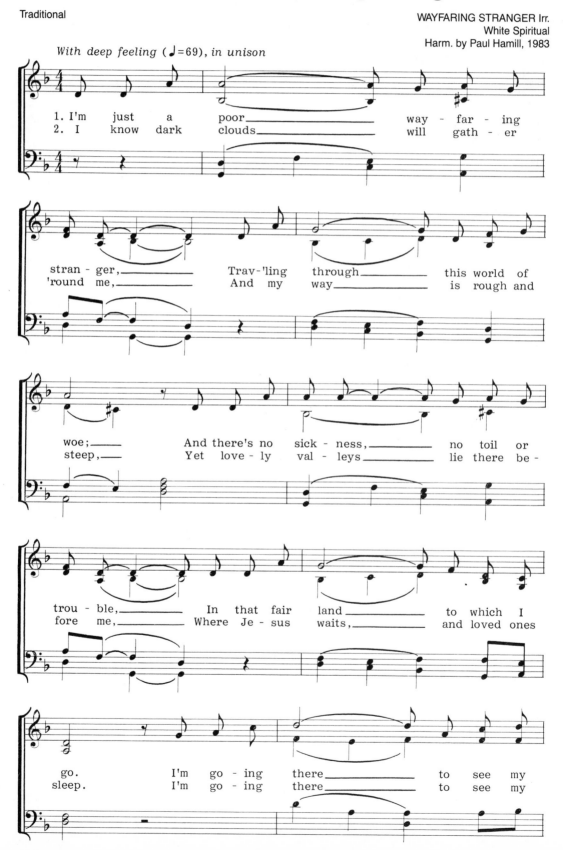

With deep feeling (♩=69), in unison

1. I'm just a poor_____ way - far - ing
2. I know dark clouds_____ will gath - er

stran - ger,_____ Trav - 'ling through_____ this world of
'round me,_____ And my way_____ is rough and

woe;_____ And there's no sick - ness,_____ no toil or
steep,_____ Yet love - ly val - leys_____ lie there be -

trou - ble,_____ In that fair land_____ to which I
fore me,_____ Where Je - sus waits,_____ and loved ones

go. I'm go - ing there_____ to see my
sleep. I'm go - ing there_____ to see my

mother, I'm go - ing there_____ no more to
Sav - ior, To sing his praise,_____ and no more

roam; I'm just a - go - ing o - ver
roam; I'm just a - go - ing o - ver

Jor - dan,____ I'm just a - go - ing o - ver home.
Jor - dan,____ I'm just a - go - ing o - ver home.

When I Am Afraid

48

Psalms 56:3
Laura Koenig, age 8
Altered, 1983

LAURA'S SONG Irr.
Laura Koenig
Harm. by M.E.H.

Simply ($\quarternote$=88), *in unison*

When I am a-fraid, a-fraid, a-fraid, When I am a-

fraid, I put my trust in You. When I am a-fraid, a-fraid, a-

fraid, When I am a-fraid, I put my trust in You.

49 O Jesus Christ, to You May Hymns Be Rising

Bradford G. Webster 1954, 1969
Altered, 1983

CITY OF GOD 11.10.11.10.
Daniel Moe, 1957

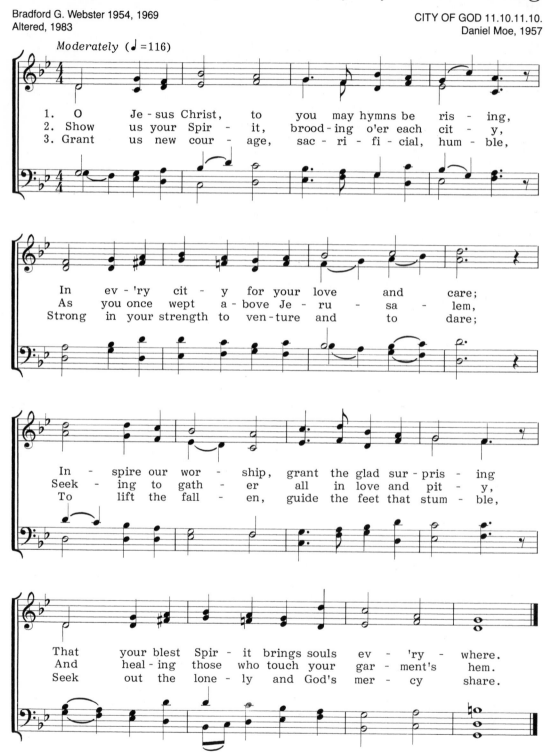

1. O Jesus Christ, to you may hymns be rising,
In ev-'ry cit-y for your love and care;
In-spire our wor-ship, grant the glad sur-pris-ing
That your blest Spir-it brings souls ev-'ry-where.

2. Show us your Spir-it, brood-ing o'er each cit-y,
As you once wept a-bove Je-ru-sa-lem,
Seek-ing to gath-er all in love and pit-y,
And heal-ing those who touch your gar-ment's hem.

3. Grant us new cour-age, sac-ri-fi-cial, hum-ble,
Strong in your strength to ven-ture and to dare;
To lift the fall-en, guide the feet that stum-ble,
Seek out the lone-ly and God's mer-cy share.

Just as we read in Luke 19:41–42 that Jesus wept over the city of Jerusalem, we, too, weep over our cities and pray that they may know healing and peace.

Gladly Now We Lift Our Voices

50

Stanza 1, F. M. Taylor, 1944, alt. 1977
Stanzas 2,3, Morris Pike, 1974, alt. 1977

SILESIA 7.7.7.7.
Silesian Melody

1. Glad - ly now we lift our voic - es Un - to
2. Ev - 'ry - one must some-times suf - fer, Ev - 'ry -
3. Ev - 'ry - one is some-times fright - ened, Some - times

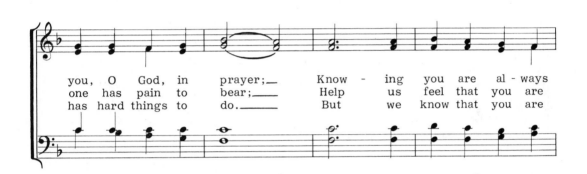

you, O God, in prayer;___ Know - ing you are al - ways
one has pain to bear;___ Help us feel that you are
has hard things to do.___ But we know that you are

with us, You are with us ev - 'ry - where.
with us, Strength - en - ing us with your care.
with us, Help - ing keep us strong and true.

Stanzas 2 and 3 from *All Our Days Laugh and Praise* by Morris D. Pike, Friendship Press, 1983. Used by permission.

51 In Our Day By Day Existence

Matthew M. Meyer

Dianne H. Rist

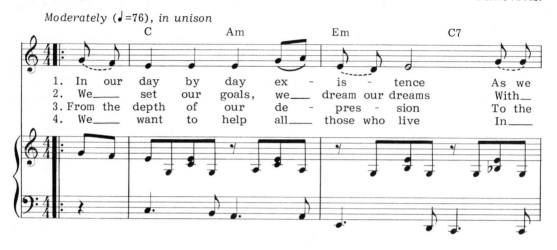

1. In our day by day exis - tence As we
2. We set our goals, we dream our dreams With
3. From the depth of our de - pres - sion To the
4. We want to help all those who live In

seek to spread your love, Help us to sense your
hopes to reach suc - cess, Help us to know that
height of hap - pi - ness, We need to know your
pale and deep de - spair. Grant us the cour - age to

pres - ence Be - neath us, a-round us, a - bove. Let the
all is lost Un - less our work you bless. Let the
grace is near To sup-port, for - give, ca - ress. Let the
lend a hand And let them know we care. Let the

52 Spirit, Spirit of Gentleness

James K. Manley

James K. Manley

In flowing style (♩=96), in unison

Spir - it, spir-it of gen-tle-ness Blow through the wil-der-ness, call-ing and free,_____ Spir - it, spir-it of rest-less-ness, Stir me from plac-id-ness, Wind, wind on the sea._____

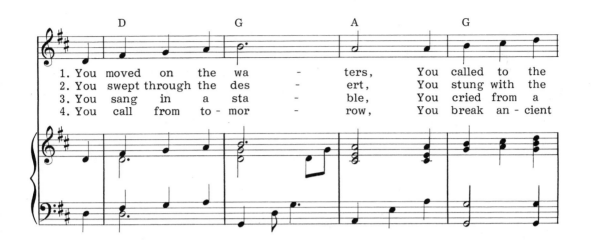

1. You moved on the wa - ters, You called to the
2. You swept through the des - ert, You stung with the
3. You sang in a sta - ble, You cried from a
4. You call from to - mor - row, You break an - cient

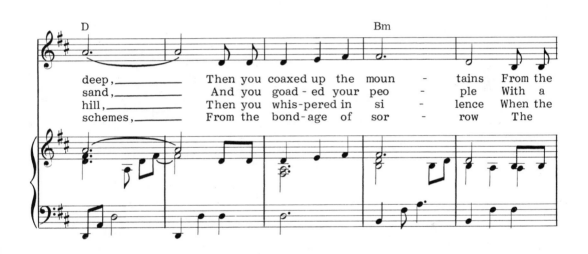

deep,_____ Then you coaxed up the moun - tains From the
sand,_____ And you goad - ed your peo - ple With a
hill,_____ Then you whis-pered in si - lence When the
schemes,_____ From the bond-age of sor - row The

val - leys of sleep,_____ And o - ver the e -
law and a land,_____ And when they were blind -
whole world was still,_____ And down in the cit -
cap - tives dream dreams;_____ Our wom - en see vi -

ons You___ called to each thing,_____
ed With their i - dols and lies,_____ Then you
y You___ called once a - gain_____ When you
sions, Our___ men clear their eyes_____ With___

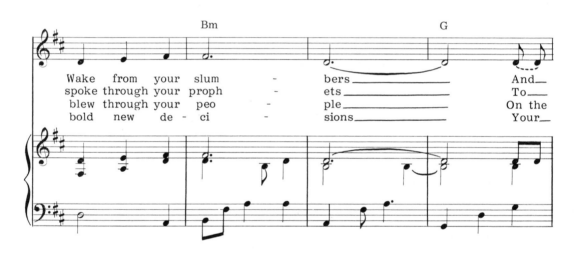

Wake from your slum - bers_____ And___
spoke through your proph - ets_____ To___
blew through your peo - ple_____ On the
bold new de - ci - sions_____ Your___

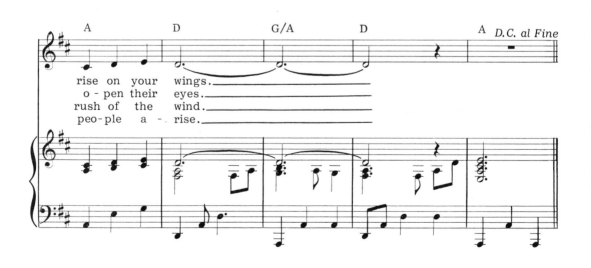

rise on your wings._____
o - pen their eyes._____
rush of the wind._____
peo-ple a - rise._____

D.C. al Fine

The Lord's My Shepherd

53

Based on Psalm 23
Scottish Psalter, 1650

BROTHER JAMES' AIR 8.6.8.6.8.6.
Melody by James Leith Macbeth Bain, c. 1840–1925
Arr. by Paul Hamill, 1983

Gently moving (♩=80), in unison

1. The Lord's my shep-herd, I'll not want, He makes me down to lie; In pas-tures green, he lead-eth me The qui-et wa - ters by. He lead-eth me, he lead-eth me, The qui - et wa - ters by.

2. My soul he doth re - store a - gain, And me to walk doth make; With - in the paths of bless - ed - ness, E'en for his own name's sake, With - in the paths of bless - ed - ness, E'en for his own name's sake.

3. Yea, though I pass through shad-owed vale, Yet will I fear no ill; For thou art with me and thy rod And staff me com - fort still. Thy rod and staff me com - fort still, Me com - fort still.

4. My ta - ble thou hast fur - nish - ed In pres - ence of my foes; My head with oil thou dost a - noint, And my cup o - ver - flows. My head thou dost with oil a - noint, And my cup o - ver - flows.

5. Good - ness and mer - cy all my days Will sure - ly fol - low me; And in my Fa - ther's heart al - ways My dwell - ing place shall be, And in my heart for - ev - er - more Thy dwell - ing place shall be.

These words could be paraphrased. For instance, the first line could be, "God is my shepherd, I'll not want, and makes me down to lie." The poignant melody, composed by James Leith Macbeth Bain, has been described as "a wonderful tune, a tune that opens its arms." The accompaniment was written especially for SING TO GOD.

Worship and Prayer

Whether we come together as two or three or in a whole congregation, we seek God's love in prayer and worship. We see the new community of love in unity with Christ in the celebration of the Lord's Supper. Through baptism or dedication of a child, the community agrees in covenant to care and nurture this child of God.

I Come With Joy to Meet My Lord

Brian A. Wren, 1971

LAND OF REST 8.6.8.6.
Southern Harmony, 1835
Arr. by Austin C. Lovelace, 1977

54

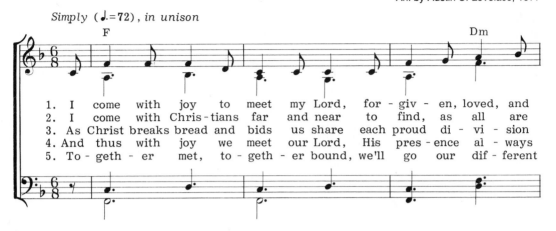

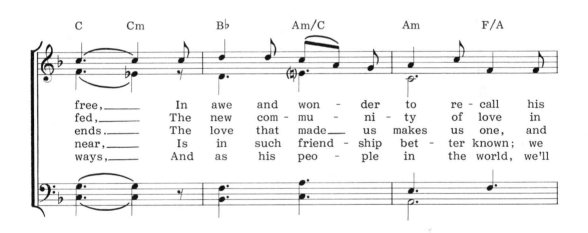

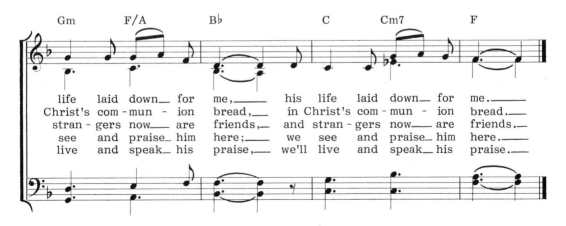

1. I come with joy to meet my Lord, for-giv-en, loved, and free,_____ In awe and won-der to re-call his life laid down__ for me,_____ his life laid down__ for me._____

2. I come with Chris-tians far and near to find, as all are fed,_____ The new com-mu-ni-ty of love in Christ's com-mun-ion bread,__ in Christ's com-mun-ion bread.__

3. As Christ breaks bread and bids us share each proud di-vi-sion ends._____ The love that made__ us makes us one, and stran-gers now__ are friends,__ and stran-gers now__ are friends.__

4. And thus with joy we meet our Lord, His pres-ence al-ways near,_____ Is in such friend-ship bet-ter known; we see and praise__ him here;__ we see and praise__ him here._____

5. To-geth-er met, to-geth-er bound, we'll go our dif-ferent ways,_____ And as his peo-ple in the world, we'll live and speak__ his praise,_____ we'll live and speak__ his praise.__

55   Kum ba Yah

Traditional

KUM BA YAH Irr.
African Slave Song

1. Kum ba-yah, my Lord, Kum ba yah! Kum ba
2. Some-one's cry-ing, Lord, Kum ba yah! Some-one's
3. Some-one's sing-ing, Lord, Kum ba yah! Some-one's
4. Some-one's pray-ing, Lord, Kum ba yah! Some-one's

yah, my Lord, Kum ba yah!   Kum ba yah, my Lord, Kum ba
cry-ing, Lord, Kum ba yah!   Some-one's cry-ing, Lord, Kum ba
sing-ing, Lord, Kum ba yah!   Some-one's sing-ing, Lord, Kum ba
pray-ing, Lord, Kum ba yah!   Some-one's pray-ing, Lord, Kum ba

yah!   Oh, Lord,__ Kum ba yah.____
yah!   Oh, Lord,__ Kum ba yah.____
yah!   Oh, Lord,__ Kum ba yah.____
yah!   Oh, Lord,__ Kum ba yah.____

It is said that the American Black spiritual, "Come by Here, Lord," was taken to Africa by American missionaries and later returned to the United States in this version (pronounced koom-bah-yah). Add some verses to this prayer, asking God to come where there is need, joy, or love.

56   Maker of All, to You We Give

Pamela-Rae Yeager Maloney, 1968

ST. MAGNUS C.M.
Jeremiah Clark, 1709

1. Mak - er of all, to you we give Our
2. We ask to - day that you a - dopt This
3. With grate - ful hearts we come to you, We

praise for birth and life; We thank you for this
child in - to your church; Send now your Spir - it
pledge to raise this child In love and trust and

won - drous gift, A new and liv - ing soul.
to be - come A pres - ent con - stant guide.
hope which is Our faith in Je - sus Christ.

Spirit of the Living God 57

Daniel Iverson

Daniel Iverson
Arr. by Herbert B. Torey

Slowly (♩ =84)

Spir - it of the liv - ing God, Fall a-fresh on me.

Fall a-fresh on me. Melt me, mold me, fill me,

use me. Spir - it of the liv-ing God, Fall a-fresh on me.

58

God, Forgive Me Now

Betty Jane Bailey

Betty Jane Bailey
Harm. by M.E.H.

Prayerfully (♩=80), in unison

1. God, for-give me now; My head is bowed; My heart is low. God, for-give me now; My head is bowed; My heart is low.
2. As a fa - ther runs To greet a son Who strayed a - way; As a wom - an search - es For a coin Lost in the dust.
3. As a shep-herd leaves To find the one That is the lost; So your love finds me, For-gives me now And brings me back.

4. God, I know your love; I raise my eyes; You lift my heart.
God, I know your love; I raise my eyes; You lift my heart.

Let Us Break Bread Together

Spiritual

LET US BREAK BREAD Irr.
Black Spiritual
Arr. by Paul Hamill, 1983

59

60 Take Our Bread We Ask You

Joseph Wise, 1967

Joseph Wise

Moderately (♩=76), in unison

Refrain

Take our bread, we ask you; take our hearts, we love you. Take our

lives, Oh Fa - ther; we are yours, we are yours. *(last time)*

Verses

Vs. 1. Yours as we stand at the ta - ble you set; yours as we

eat the bread our hearts can't for - get. We are the sign of your

(Repeat Refrain)

life with us yet, we are yours, we are yours. Take our

Vs. 2. Your ho - ly peo - ple stand - ing washed in your blood. Spir - it filled yet

hun - gry we a - wait your food. We are poor, but we've brought our - selves

(Repeat Refrain)

the best we could; we are yours, we are yours. Take our

Instead of "Oh, Father," one might sing, "Oh, Maker."

Our Father Who Art in Heaven

Based on Matthew 6:9–13

WEST INDIES TUNE Irr.
Collected by Olive Pattison, 1945
Arr. by Paul Abels, 1964

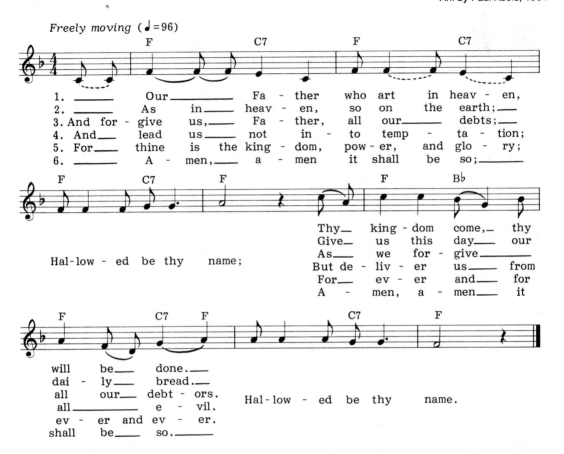

Freely moving (♩=96)

1. _____ Our_____ Fa - ther who art in heav - en,
2. _____ As in_____ heav - en, so on the earth;_____
3. And for - give us,_____ Fa - ther, all our_____ debts;_____
4. And_____ lead us_____ not in - to temp - ta - tion;
5. For_____ thine is the king - dom, pow - er, and glo - ry;
6. _____ A - men,_____ a - men it shall be so;_____

Hal-low - ed be thy name;

Thy_ king - dom come,_ thy
Give_ us this day_____ our
As_ we for - give_____
But de - liv - er us_____ from
For_ ev - er and_ for
A - men, a - men_____ it

F   C7   F   C7   F

will be_ done._
dai - ly_ bread._
all our_ debt - ors.
all_____ e - vil.
ev - er and ev - er.
shall be_ so._____

Hal-low - ed be thy name.

This West Indies version of the familiar and loved Lord's Prayer can be sung by a soloist with the group responding, "Hallowed be thy name." The words could be adapted. For instance, stanza 5 might be, "For yours is the realm, the power, and glory . . . ."

62 Not My Brother, Not My Sister

Traditional

IT'S ME, O LORD Irr.
Black Spiritual
Harm. by Paul Hamill, 1983

Not my broth-er, not my sis-ter but it's me, O, Lord,

1. Stand-ing in the need of prayer.

2. Stand-ing in the need of

Chorus

prayer. It's me, It's me, O, Lord, Stand-ing in the need of

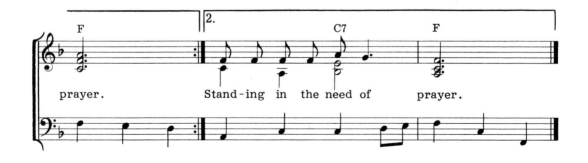

1. prayer.

2. Stand-ing in the need of prayer.

Jesus: Advent

In the season of Advent, we seek God's presence and prepare for the joyful Christmastide. We remember the prophecies and the good news that are ours to share. We pray for light to come into our lives this season.

63   O Come, O Come, Emmanuel

Latin: c. 9th Century
Stanza 1, Tr. John M. Neale, 1818–1866, Alt.
Stanza 2, Tr. Henry S. Coffin, 1877–1954

VENI EMMANUEL 8.8.8.8.8.8.
Melody adapted from Plainsong, Mode I
Thomas Helmore, 1854

Freely (♩=120), *in unison*

1. O come, O come, Em - man - u - el, And ran - som cap - tive
2. O come, De - sire of na - tions, bind All peo - ples in one

Is - ra - el, That mourns in lone - ly ex - ile___ here, Un -
heart and mind; Bid en - vy, strife and quar - rels___ cease; Fill

in harmony

til the Son of God___ ap - pear. Re - joice! Re - joice! Em -
the whole world with heav - en's peace.

man - u - el Shall come to thee, O Is - ra - el!

The present hymn is based on Neale's translation as it appeared in revised form in his *Hymnal Noted,* 1854. Thomas Helmore (1811–1890) is credited with arranging the tune from phrases of plainsong settings of the "Kyrie."

Comfort, Comfort All My People

Isaiah 40:1–8
Johann Olearins, 1671
Tr. Catherine Winkworth, 1827–1878
Adapted by Mary N. Hawkes, 1983

WERDE MUNTER, MEIN GEMÜTE 8.7.8.7.77.8.8.
Johann Schop, 1642

Moderately (♩=96)

1. Com - fort,_ com - fort all my peo - ple, Tell of peace, thus
2. Hark, the_ mes - sen - ger is cry - ing In the des - ert
3. So make_ straight what long was crook - ed, Make the rough - er

says our God; Com - fort_ those who sit in dark - ness
far and near, Bid - ding_ all to their re - pen - tance
pla - ces_ plain; Let your_ hearts be true and hum - ble,

Mourn-ing 'neath their sor-rows' load. To Je - ru - sa - lem, O say
Since the king - dom now is here. Oh, that warn-ing cry o - bey!
As be - fits God's ho - ly reign. For the glo - ry of our God

That new peace will come its way; Say that_ God all
Now pre - pare for God a way; Ev - 'ry_ val - ley
Now o'er earth is shed a - broad; And all_ flesh shall

sins will cov - er, And that war - fare now is o - ver.
shall be ris - ing, And the hills to God be bow - ing.
see the to - ken That God's word is nev - er_ bro - ken.

Light the Advent Candle

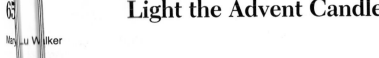

Mary Lu Walker
Arr. by H. Myron Braun

Not too fast (♩=96), in unison

1. Light the Ad - vent can - dle, one: Now the wait - ing
2. Light the Ad - vent can - dle, two: Think of hum - ble
3. Light the Ad - vent can - dle, three: Think of heav'n - ly
4. Light the Ad - vent can - dle, four: Think of joy for -
5. Light the Christ - mas can - dles, now: Sing of don - key,

has be - gun; We have start - ed on our
shep - herds, who Filled with won - der at the
har - mo - ny; An - gels sing - ing "Peace on
ev - er - more; Christ - child in a sta - ble
sheep, and cow; Birth - day can - dles for the

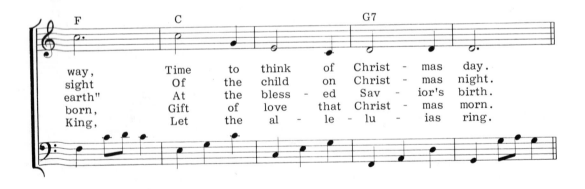

way, Time to think of Christ - mas day.
sight Of the child on Christ - mas night.
earth" At the bless - ed Sav - ior's birth.
born, Gift of love that Christ - mas morn.
King, Let the al - le - lu - ias ring.

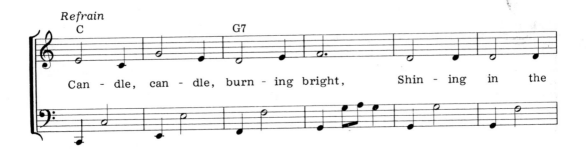

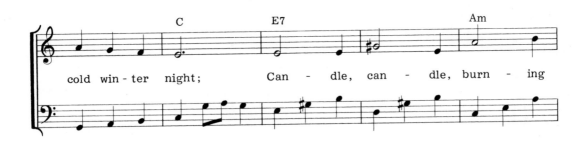

66 My Soul Magnifies the Lord

Luke 1: 46–55
Adaptation by Ewald Bash

MAGNIFICAT Irr.
Ewald Bash
Arr. by Paul Abels

Freely (♩.=60), in unison

1. My soul____ mag - ni - fies____ the Lord, And my
2. His mer - cy is on____ those who wor - ship Him; His chil -
3. He has helped His ser - vant Is - ra - el In re -

spir - it re - joic - es in God.____ For
dren in each gen - er - a - tion.____ And
mem - brance of His mer - cy;____ As He

He has re - gard - ed the low - li - ness Of this
strong is His arm as He scat - ters the proud In the
spake to our Fa - thers, to A - bra - ham, And to

poor____ maid - en. Be -
van - i - ty of____ their hearts.____ He
His____ chil - dren____ for - ev - er. Glo -

In this beautiful hymn, "The Magnificat," Mary is expressing her own humility and her praise of God. Take the same thought and write new words to this tune.

67 O Lift Your Heads, You Mighty Gates

Georg Weissel, 1642
Tr. Catherine Winkworth, 1827–1878
Adapted by Mary N. Hawkes, 1983

MACHT HOCH DIE TÜR L.M.
German Chorale

With joyful dignity (♩ =108)

1. O lift your heads, you might-y gates, Be-hold the King of
2. O blest the land, the cit-y blest, Where Christ the lead-er
3. Fling wide the por-tals of your heart; Make it a tem-ple,

Glo-ry waits; The King of kings soon will be here, The
is con-fessed! O hap-py hearts and hap-py homes To
set a-part From world-ly use for love's em-ploy, A-

Sav-ior of the world draws near. Sal-va-tion, life, and
whom this King in tri-umph comes! An end to all in-
dorned with prayer, and love, and joy; So shall your lead-er

joy he brings To all the world which glad-ly sings Its
jus-tice brings To all the world which glad-ly sings Its
en-ter in, And new and no-bler life be-gin, O

praise to God a-bove, Cre-a-tor, wis-dom, love.
praise to God a-bove, Cre-a-tor, wis-dom, love.
praise to God a-bove, Cre-a-tor, wis-dom, love.

People in Darkness Are Looking for Light   68

Dosia Carlson

ADVENT HYMN Irr.
Dosia Carlson, 1983

Gently moving (♩.=66), in unison

1. Peo - ple in dark-ness are look-ing for light, Come, come, come Je - sus Christ; Peo-ple with blind-ness are long-ing for sight, Come, Lord Je - sus Christ.___ These days of ad - ven-ture when all peo - ple wait are days for the ad - vent of Love.

2. Peo - ple with sick-ness are pray-ing for health, Come, come, come Je - sus Christ; Peo-ple in pov - er - ty want to have wealth, Come, Lord Je - sus Christ.___ These days of ad - ven-ture when all peo - ple wait are days for the ad - vent of Hope.

3. Peo - ple in trou - ble would like to be free, Come, come, come Je - sus Christ; Peo-ple with ar - gu-ments want to a - gree, Come, Lord Je - sus Christ.___ These days of ad - ven-ture when all peo - ple wait are days for the ad - vent of Peace.

69 Hey! Hey! Anybody Listening

Richard Avery

Donald Marsh

This song is welcoming Jesus to our midst with enthusiasm, welcoming the Advent season but also proclaiming Jesus' birth and life. It is calling us to witness to and tell the good news.

Jesus: Birth

We celebrate the birth of Jesus, the coming of the shepherds and the homage of the kings who gave their love in wonder and joy. We, too, may feel wonder and joy anew. We, too, may bring our gifts.

Go, Tell It on the Mountain

Spiritual

GO, TELL IT ON THE MOUNTAIN Irr.
Black Spiritual
Harm. by Paul Hamill, 1983

Moderately fast (♩=116), in unison

Refrain

Go, tell it on the moun - tain,

O - ver the hills and ev - 'ry - where; Go tell it on the

moun - tain That Je - sus Christ is born!

Fine

Slightly slower (♩=100), in harmony

1. While shep-herds kept their watch-ing O'er si - lent flocks by night, Be-
2. The shep-herds feared and trem-bled When lo! a - bove the earth Rang
3. Down in a low - ly man-ger The hum-ble Christ was born, And

D.C.

hold through-out the heav-ens There shone a ho - ly light.__
out the an - gel cho - rus That hailed our Sav - ior's birth.__
God sent us sal - va - tion That bless - ed Christ-mas morn.__

71   I Wonder as I Wander

Appalachian Carol

I WONDER AS I WANDER Irr.
Appalachian Carol
John Jacob Niles
Harm. by Paul Hamill, 1983

Quietly (♪=92), in unison

1. I won - der as I wan - der, out un - der the sky, How
2. When Mar - y birthed Je - sus, 'twas in a cow's stall, With
3. If Je - sus had want - ed for an - y wee thing, A
4. I won - der as I wan - der, out un - der the sky, How

Je - sus the Sav - ior did come for to die For
wise men and farm - ers and shep - herds and all. But
star in the sky or a bird on the wing, Or
Je - sus the Sav - ior did come for to die For

poor or - nery peo - ple like you and like I; I
high from God's heav - en a star's light did fall, The
all of God's an - gels in heav'n for to sing, He
poor or - nery peo - ple like you and like I; I

won - der as I wan - der, out un - der the sky.
prom - ise of a - ges it did then re - call.
sure - ly could have it, 'cause he was the King.
won - der as I wan - der out un - der the sky.

This tune was collected by the folk singer, arranger, and composer, John Jacob Niles. This lovely carol was sung originally in the Southern Appalachian Mountains.

Jesus the Christ Is Born

Appalachian Carol
Adapted, 1983

Southern Appalachian Carol
John Jacob Niles

72

Simply (♩=76), in unison

1. Je - sus the Christ is born, Give
2. You might - y kings of earth, Be -
3. Je - sus the Christ is born, Give

thanks now, ev - 'ry one. Re - joice, you great ones
fore the man - ger bed, Cast down, cast down your
thanks now, ev - 'ry one. Re - joice, you great ones

and you small, God's will, it has been done.
gold - en crown From off your roy - al head.
and you small, God's will, it has been done.

73 Jesus, My Babe, Sleep Quietly

Phyllis C. White

LE P'ING Irr.
Chinese Folk Melody

Simply (♩=84), in unison

Je - sus, my babe, sleep qui - et - ly, In ear - ly morn - ing chill; The shep - herds came to sing your praise; Their words are with me still. Who you are and what you shall be On - ly God can_ know; Each day will bring some - thing new, New things that help you grow.

Mary Had a Baby, Yes, God

Stanza 1, Traditional American
Stanzas 2, 3, Ruth Crawford Seeger
Adapted by Mary N. Hawkes, 1983

JESUS IN A MANGER Irr.
American Carol
Harm. by Paul Hamill, 1983

74

Gently moving (♩ = 120), in unison

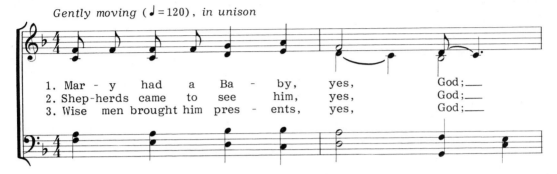

1. Mar - y had a Ba - by, yes, God;___
2. Shep - herds came to see him, yes, God;___
3. Wise men brought him pres - ents, yes, God;___

Mar - y had a Ba - by, O yes, God;
Shep - herds came to see him, O yes, God;
Wise men brought him pres - ents, O yes, God;

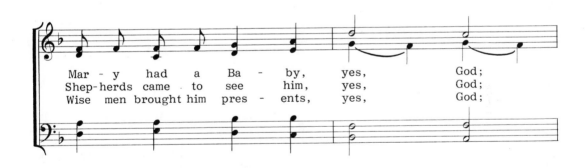

Mar - y had a Ba - by, yes, God;
Shep - herds came to see him, yes, God;
Wise men brought him pres - ents, yes, God;

Je - sus in a man - ger at Beth - le - hem.
Je - sus in a man - ger at Beth - le - hem.
Je - sus in a man - ger at Beth - le - hem.

75 'Twas in the Moon of Wintertime

Huron Indian Words
St. Jean de Brébeaf, 1593–1649
Tr. by J. Edgar Middleton, 1872–1960
Adapted by Mary N. Hawkes, 1983

JESUS AHATONHIA Irr.
Huron Indian Carol
Arr. by Healey Willan, 1880–1968

1. 'Twas in the moon of win-ter-time, When all the birds had fled, That might-y Git-chi
Man-i-tou Sent an-gel choirs in-stead; Be-fore their light the

(2.) bro-ken bark The ten-der babe was found, A rag-ged robe of
rab-bit skin En-wrapped his beau-ty round; But as the hun-ter

(3.) win-ter-time Is not so round and fair As was the ring of
glo-ry on The help-less in-fant there. The chiefs from far be-

(4.) for-est free, O heirs of Man-i-tou, The Ho-ly Child of
earth and heaven Is born to-day for you. Come kneel be-fore the

This beautiful Huron Indian melody was arranged by Healey Willan, distinguished Canadian church musician. Willan was organist and professor of music at the University of Toronto. He was also a prolific composer of chamber and orchestral compositions.

76

O Come, Little Children

Christoph von Schmid, 1769–1854

Johann A.P. Schulz, 1747–1800

1. O come, lit - tle chil - dren, O come, one and all! O come to the cra - dle in Beth - le - hem's stall; The bright star will guide us and show us the way To

2. O look in the cra - dle How sweet and how small, O see how the bright star shines o - ver the stall! His moth - er has dressed him, the heav - en - ly child. And

3. The an - i - mals all seem to know Mar - y's boy, And Jo - seph, with Mar - y, be - holds him with joy; The shep - herds have en - tered to him love they bring, While

4. O come with the shep - herds, O come to the stall, With hearts full of love for the one who loves all! O sing, lit - tle chil - dren, to him you a - dore; ___

Je - sus who's ly - ing a - sleep on the hay.
an - gels pro - claim him, so sweet and so mild!
an - gels sing joy - ous - ly, mer - ri - ly sing!
Sing with the an - gels sing peace ev - er - more!

Words and music of "O Come, Little Children" by Christoph von Schmid and Johann A. P. Schulz from *A Book of Christmas Carols* selected by Haig and Regina Shekerjian. Arranged for piano with guitar chords by Robert De Cormier. Copyright © 1963, 1977, by Haig and Regina Shekerjian. Reprinted by permission of Harper & Row, Publishers, Inc.

Little Baby Jesus

77

Mary Voell Jones

Mary Voell Jones

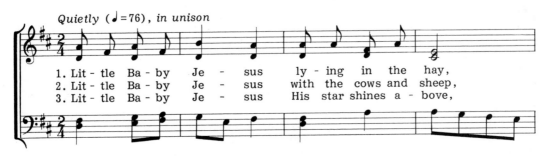

Quietly (♩ =76), in unison

1. Lit - tle Ba - by Je - sus ly - ing in the hay,
2. Lit - tle Ba - by Je - sus with the cows and sheep,
3. Lit - tle Ba - by Je - sus His star shines a - bove,

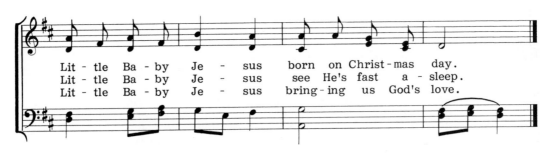

Lit - tle Ba - by Je - sus born on Christ - mas day.
Lit - tle Ba - by Je - sus see He's fast a - sleep.
Lit - tle Ba - by Je - sus bring - ing us God's love.

"Little Baby Jesus" from *Let's Make Music Today* by Mary Voell Jones. © 1977 by Mary Voell Jones. Used by permission of Paulist Press.

78　Jesus Our Brother, Strong and Good

Robert Davis, 1881–1950
Altered, 1983

FRIENDLY BEASTS Irr.
Medieval French Melody
Attr. to Pierre de Corbeil

1. Je - sus our Broth - er, ___ strong ___ and good,
2. I, said the don - key, ___ shag - gy and brown,
3. I, said the cow, all ___ white ___ and red,
4. I, said the sheep, with ___ cur - ly horn,
5. I, said the dove, from the raft - ers high,
6. So ev - 'ry beast by ___ some ___ good spell

Was ___ hum - bly born ___ in a sta - ble rude,
I ___ car - ried his moth - er up ___ hill ___ and down,
I ___ gave him my man - ger for ___ his bed,
I ___ gave him my wool ___ for his blan - ket warm,
I ___ cooed him to sleep ___ that he should ___ not cry.
In the sta - ble dark ___ was ___ glad ___ to tell

And the friend - ly beasts ___ a - round ___ him stood,
I ___ car - ried her safe - ly to Beth - le - hem town;
I ___ gave him my hay ___ to pil - low his head;
He ___ wore ___ my coat ___ on Christ - mas morn;
We ___ cooed him to sleep, ___ my mate ___ and I;
Of the gift ___ it gave ___ Em - man - u - el,

Je - sus our Broth - er, ___ strong ___ and good.
I, said the don - key, ___ shag - gy and brown.
I, said the cow, all ___ white ___ and red.
I, said the sheep, with ___ cur - ly horn.
I, said the dove, from the raft - ers high.
The gift it gave Em - man - u - el.

Once for Us a Boy Was Born

W. Lawrence Curry, 1939
Adapted by Mary N. Hawkes, 1983

PUER NOBIS NASCITUR
From *Piae Cantiones,* 1582
Harm. by W. Lawrence Curry, 1939

79

Moderately (♩=126), in unison

1. Once for us a Boy was born, Joy and glad - ness
2. In the fields the shep - herds lay, Watch - ing sheep so
3. As the three kings did of old, So we bring our
4. Come, let's all sing praise to God Who brought a - bout this

bring - ing; Long a - go on Christ - mas morn, Both
low - ly; Till in vast and bright ar - ray Ap -
treas - ure; Gifts of self as well as gold To
glo - ry; Sing we now in great - est joy Sal -

heaven and earth were sing - ing__ Praise to God in heav - en!
peared the an - gels ho - ly.__ Praise to God in heav - en!
him in full - est meas - ure.__ Praise to God in heav - en!
va - tion's glo - rious sto - ry,__ Praise to God in heav - en!

80 Why Is the Night so Still

Kenneth I. Morse

Wilbur E. Brumbaugh

Gently moving (♩=96), in unison

1. Why is the night so___ still, so___ ho - ly?
2. Why do the heav - ens___ fill with___ mu - sic?

Why have the shep - herds come to town?
What do these an - gel voic - es tell?

They come to see a child born low - ly
They sing of Christ, the world's re - deem - er.

1. Here in a man - ger___ bed - ded___ down.

2. God in our midst, Im - man - u - el.

Once in Royal David's City

81

Cecil F. Alexander, 1849
Adapted by Mary N. Hawkes, 1983

IRBY 8.7.8.7.7.7
Henry J. Gauntlett, 1858

1. Once in roy-al Da-vid's cit-y Stood a low-ly cat-tle shed Where a moth-er laid her Ba-by In a man-ger for his bed: Mar-y was that moth-er mild, Je-sus Christ, her lit-tle Child.

2. He came bring-ing peace on earth, In him came God's love for all, And his shel-ter was a sta-ble, And his cra-dle was a stall: With the poor, and mean, and low-ly, Lived on earth our Sav-iour ho-ly.

82   What Child Is This, Who, Laid to Rest

William Chatterton Dix, 1861
Adapted, 1983

GREENSLEEVES 8.7.8.7. with refrain
17th Century English Melody

Gently (♩.=58)

1. What child is this,—who, laid to rest,— On Mar-y's lap—is sleep-ing?
2. Why lies he in—such mean es-tate,—Where ox and ass—are feed-ing?
3. So bring him in - cense, gold, and myrrh;—Come, rich and poor,—to own him.

Whom an-gels greet—with an-thems sweet,—While shep-herds watch—are keep-ing?
Good Chris-tian, fear,—for sin-ners here—The si - lent Word—is plead-ing.
The King of kings—sal-va - tion brings;—Let lov - ing hearts—en-throne him.

This,   this—is Christ the King,— Whom shep-herds guard—and an - gels sing!

Haste,   haste—to bring him laud,—The Babe,—the Son—of Mar - y!

"Greensleeves" is a traditional English ballad tune that has been sung to many different sets of words. The tune was mentioned by Shakespeare and other writers of this time. Some versions of it have a C sharp in measures one and five of the refrain; however, the C natural seems to be the most authentic.

We've Been a While A'Wandering

Yorkshire Carol
Adapted by Mary N. Hawkes, 1983

Yorkshire Carol
Arr. Olaf C. Christiansen, 1952

83

Briskly (♩.= 86), in unison

1. We've been a while a 'wan-der-ing A-mong the leaves so
2. God bless all a-ges in this house, All grown-ups, young and

green,___ But now we come a-car-ol-ing So plain-ly to be
old,___ And all young folks and chil-dren Be-long-ing to our

seen;}
fold;} For it's Christ-mas time When we trav-el far and

near, May God bless you and send you A hap-py New___ Year.___

In this lovely folk carol, we sing of the beautiful Christmas event but also express our hope that God will bring the listener a happy new year.

84 Wasn't That a Mighty Day

Black Spiritual

MIGHTY DAY Irr.
Black Spiritual

Moderately fast (♩=104), in unison

Was-n't that a might-y day? Hal-le - lu!_ Hal-le - lu-jah!

Was-n't that a might-y day When Je - sus Christ was born?

From *The Whole World Singing,* compiled by Edith Lovell Thomas, Friendship Press, 1950. Used by permission.

Add some new verses to this spiritual, for instance, "Wasn't that a mighty day—when shepherds came to see."

85 To Jesus From the Ends of Earth

Huron Indian Carol
Translated by Ruth Heller
Altered

JESUS AHATONHIA Irr.
Huron Indian Carol
Arr. by Roberta Bitgood

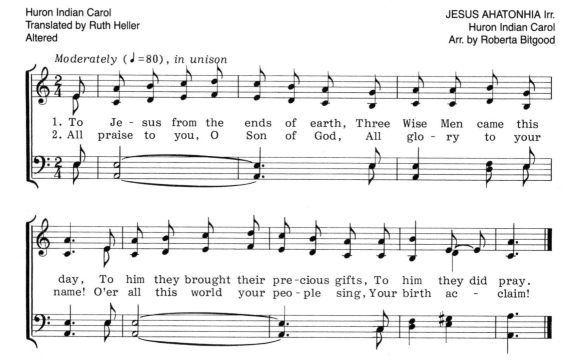

Moderately (♩=80), in unison

1. To Je - sus from the ends of earth, Three Wise Men came this
2. All praise to you, O Son of God, All glo - ry to your

day, To him they brought their pre-cious gifts, To him they did pray.
name! O'er all this world your peo - ple sing, Your birth ac - claim!

Music copyright, 1946, by The Westminster Press; renewed, 1974; from *Hymns for Primary Worship.* Used by permission.

The Wise May Bring Their Learning   86

Anonymous
From *The Book of Praise for Children,* 1881
Adapted by Mary N. Hawkes, 1983

CLONMEL, C.M.D.
Irish Melody
Harm. by Paul Hamill, 1983

1. The wise may bring their learning. The rich may bring their wealth. And some may bring their greatness, And some bring strength and health; We, too, would bring our treasures To offer to the King: We have no wealth or learning; What shall we to him bring?

2. We'll bring hearts filled with loving; We'll bring our thankful praise! While always humbly striving; To follow in his ways. Far better are these treasures We offer to the King, Than richest gifts without them; Yet these we each may bring.

In the good news of Jesus' coming, material riches and power do not matter. What does matter is bringing our love to share with others no matter what our age may be. How may we share our love with others?

87 This Highway, Beheld at Break of Day

Edward Bliss Reed
Adapted by Mary N. Hawkes, 1983

From the French

Majestically (♩ =96)

This high-way,__ be-held at break of day,__ Three East-ern

kings in full ar-ray are march-ing. This high-way,__ be-held at break of

day,__ They to the new-born child are on their way. With gifts of

gold, frank-in-cense and myrrh____ They come their

treas-ures to bring from far a-way,____ With gifts of

gold, frank-in-cense and myrrh,__ With pride they hom-age to the child do

1. pay.   2. pay.

88 Now the Kings Are Coming

Puerto Rican Carol
English Paraphrase by Miriam L. Transue, 1957

THE GREAT KINGS Irr.
Puerto Rican Carol
Acc. by Miriam L. Transue, 1957

Moderately (♩=80), *in unison*

1.   2.

Now the Kings are com - ing,__ The great Kings__ from far.
Los tres San - tos Re - yes,__ los tres, y__ los tres,

Now the Kings are com - ing,__ The great Kings__ from far.
los tres San - tos Re - yes,__ los tres, y__ los tres,

From the O - rient rid - ing,__ They fol - low__ a star.
los sa - lu - da - re - mos,__ con di - vi - na fé,

Stanza 1.   Stanza 2.

From the O - rient rid - ing,__ They fol - low__ a star.
los sa - lu - da - re - mos,__ con di - vi - na fé.

Words and music from *Christmas Songs from Puerto Rico,* by Miriam L. Transue; Commonwealth of Puerto Rico, 1957.

Joy to the World

89

Psalms 98:5–9
Isaac Watts, 1719, alt.
Adapted by Ruth C. Duck

ANTIOCH C.M.
Attr. to George F. Handel, 1742
Arr. by Lowell Mason, 1839

1. Joy to the world! The prom-ised one has come sha-lom to bring. Let ev-'ry heart pre-pare a room, And heav'n and na-ture sing, And heav'n and na-ture sing, And heav'n, and heav'n and na-ture sing.

2. Joy to the world! The Sav-ior reigns: Let all their songs em-ploy; While fields and floods, rocks, hills, and plains Re-peat the sound-ing joy, Re-peat the sound-ing joy, Re-peat, re-peat the sound-ing joy.

3. Grace-ful and true, The Sav-ior rules, And makes the na-tions prove The glo-ries of the ways of peace, And won-ders of God's love, And won-ders of God's love, And won-ders, won-ders of God's love.

Jesus: Life and Ministry

Throughout Jesus' life, in his childhood and in his adult relationships with his followers, we see his love for all persons. Some misunderstood his message and put him to death, but his loving relationships with all, including children, shine through in his healing, teaching, and traveling throughout the land. As Jesus inspired persons and brought joy to them, he inspires us and brings us joy.

ΙΧΘΥC

We Would See Jesus

J. Edgar Park, 1879–1956
Altered, 1983

SOUTH CHURCH 11.10.11.10.
Paul Hamill, 1983

90

Moderately (♩=84), in unison

1. We would see Je - sus; lo! his star is shin - ing
2. We would see Je - sus; Ma - ry's son most ho - ly,
3. We would see Je - sus; on the moun-tain teach - ing,
4. We would see Je - sus; in his work of heal - ing,
5. We would see Je - sus; in the ear - ly morn - ing,

A - bove the sta - ble while the an - gels sing;
Light of the vil - lage life from day to day;
With all the lis - tening peo - ple gath - ered round;
At e - ven - tide be - fore the sun was set;
To fol - low him he calls as in past days;

in harmony

There in a man - ger on the hay re - clin - ing,
Shin - ing re - vealed through ev - 'ry task most low - ly,
While birds and flowers and sky a - bove are preach - ing
Di - vine and hu - man, in his deep re - veal - ing,
Let us a - rise, all mean - er ser - vice scorn - ing;

Haste, let us lay our gifts be - fore the king.
The Christ of God, the life, the truth, the way.
The bless - ed - ness which sim - ple trust has found.
Per - son and God in lov - ing ser - vice met.
And give our lives to him in lov - ing ways.

91   O Sing a Song of Bethlehem

Louis F. Benson, 1899

NOEL C.M.D.
English Melody
Harm. by Paul Hamill, 1983

In moderate time (♩=104), in unison

1. O__ sing a song of__ Beth-le-hem, Of shep-herds watch-ing there,
2. O__ sing a song of__ Naz-a-reth, Of sun-ny days__ of joy,
3. O__ sing a song of__ Gal-i-lee, Of lake and woods__ and hill,
4. O__ sing a song of__ Cal-va-ry, Its glo-ry and__ dis-may;

And__ of the news that came to them From__ an-gels in the air:
O__ sing of fra-grant flow-ers' breath, And__ of__ the sin-less boy:
Of__ him who walked up-on the sea And__ bade_ its waves be still:
Of__ him who hung up-on the tree, And__ took_ our sins a-way:

The light that shone on Beth-le-hem Fills all the world to-day;
For now the flowers of Naz-a-reth In ev-'ry heart may grow;
For though, like waves on Gal-i lee, Dark seas of trou-ble roll,
For he who died on Cal-va-ry Is ris-en from the grave,

Of Je-sus' birth and_ peace on earth The_ an-gels sing al-way.
Now spreads the fame of__ his dear name On__ all__ the winds that blow.
When faith has heard the_ liv-ing word, Falls_ peace_ up-on the soul.
And Christ, our Lord, by_ heaven a-dored, Is__ might-y now to save.

Amen

Black Spiritual
Altered, 1983

AMEN Irr.
Black Spiritual
Arr. by Marion Downs

1. See the ba - by,
2. See him in the temple,
3. See him at the seaside,
4. See him in the garden,
5. Yes, he is our Savior,

Ly - ing in a man-ger   One Christ - mas morn - ing.
Talk - ing to the Eld - ers,   How they marvelled at his wisdom.
Preach - ing and heal - ing,   To the blind and the feeble.
Pray - ing to his Mak - er   In deep - est sor - row.
Je - sus died to save us,   And he rose on Easter.

6. Hal - le - lu - jah   In the king -

dom with my Sav - ior.   A - men, A - men!

A - men,   A - men, A - men, A - men!

93 At Work Beside His Father's Bench

Alice M. Pullen

KINGSFOLD C.M.D.
English Melody
Arr. Ralph Vaughan Williams, 1872–1958

With spirit (♩=108)

1. At___ work be - side his fa - ther's bench, At___
2. And___ in the lit - tle flat - roofed house He___
3. Through hard - ships and through dan - gers too, Un -

play when work___ was done; In___ qui - et Gal - i -
served with will - ing hand; His___ moth - er's dai - ly
daunt - ed, tire - less, brave; For___ trou - bled, sick, and

lee he lived, The___ Friend of ev - 'ry - one.
bur - dens bore, Her___ joys and pleas - ures planned.
wea - ry friends His___ dai - ly life___ he gave.

Com - rade of boys___ and girls like us, Play -
And___ as he grew___ to be a man, He___
And___ when he left___ his faith - ful friends, To___

mate so___ straight and true, In___ all our work,___ in___
wan - dered___ far and wide, To___ be a Friend to___
do God's___ work and will, He___ prom - ised them___ he'd___

all our play, Make us true com - rades too.
ev - 'ry - one Through - out the coun - try - side.
be, un - seen, Their faith - ful Com - rade still.

I Wish I Had Known Jesus 94

Mary Alice Murray, 1976

MEIN LEBEN 7.6.7.6.
Melody by Melchior Vulpius, c. 1560–1616

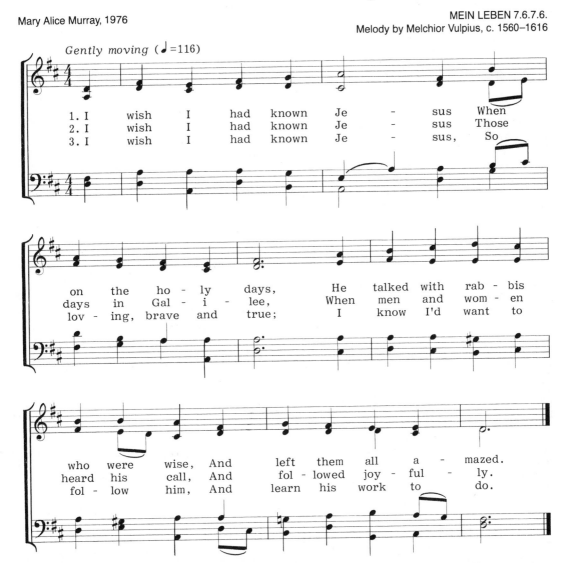

Gently moving (♩=116)

1. I wish I had known Je - sus When
2. I wish I had known Je - sus Those
3. I wish I had known Je - sus, So

on the ho - ly days, He talked with rab - bis
days in Gal - i - lee, When men and wom - en
lov - ing, brave and true; I know I'd want to

who were wise, And left them all a - mazed.
heard his call, And fol - lowed joy - ful - ly.
fol - low him, And learn his work to do.

95 Jesus Was a Loving Teacher

Wilhelmina D'A. Stephens, 1945
Altered, 1979, 1983

CROSS OF JESUS 8.7.8.7.
John Stainer, 1840–1901

Moderately slow (♩=100)

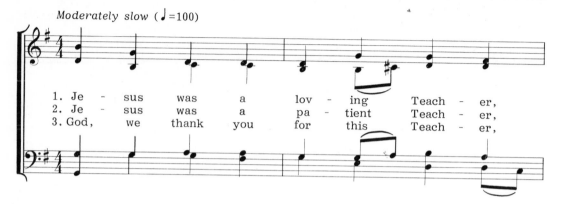

1. Je - sus was a lov - ing Teach - er,
2. Je - sus was a pa - tient Teach - er,
3. God, we thank you for this Teach - er,

Help - ing peo - ple day by day;___ Know the love of
Want - ing all___ to learn God's will,___ Tell - ing sto - ries
And our praise to you we give,___ For his love and

God our Mak - er, Teach - ing them___ to love and pray.
they'd re - mem - ber, Sto - ries that___ we're read - ing still.
for his pa - tience, Show - ing peo - ple how to live.

Often Jesus' Friends Remembered

Ellen E. Fraser, 1944

STUTTGART 8.7.8.7.
Adapted from a melody by Christian Friedrich Witt

Moderately fast (♩ =104)

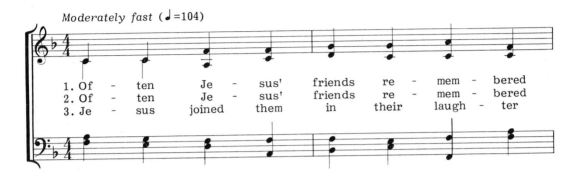

1. Of - ten Je - sus' friends re - mem - bered
2. Of - ten Je - sus' friends re - mem - bered
3. Je - sus joined them in their laugh - ter

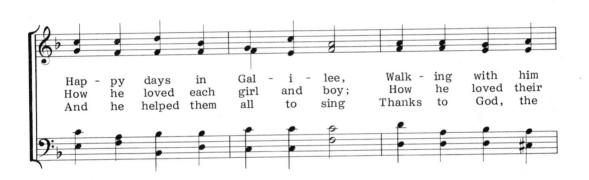

Hap - py days in Gal - i - lee, Walk - ing with him
How he loved each girl and boy; How he loved their
And he helped them all to sing Thanks to God, the

through the mead - ow, Walk - ing down be - side the sea.
hap - py laugh - ter, How he loved their songs of joy.
great Cre - a - tor Of each good and love - ly thing.

97

O Young and Fearless Prophet

S. Ralph Harlow
Altered, 1983

NYLAND 7.6.7.6.D.
Finnish Melody
Harm. by David Evans, 1874–1948

In moderate time ($\quarternote$ =108)

1. O young and fear-less Proph - et Of an-cient Gal - i - lee,
2. We mar - vel at the pur - pose That held you to your course
3. Cre - ate in us the splen - dor That dawns when hearts are kind,
4. O young and fear-less Proph - et, We need your pres-ence here,

Your life is still a sum - mons To serve hu - man - i - ty,
While ev - er on the hill - top Be - fore you loomed the cross;
That knows not race nor sta - tion As bound-aries of the mind;
A - mid our pride and glo - ry To see your face ap - pear;

To make our thoughts and ac - tions Less prone to please the crowd,
Your stead-fast face set for - ward Where love and du - ty shone,
That learns to val - ue beau - ty, In heart, or brain, or soul.
Once more to hear your chal-lenge A - bove our nois - y day,

To stand with hum - ble cour - age For truth, with hearts un - cowed.
While we be - tray so quick - ly And leave you there a - lone.
And longs to bind God's chil - dren In - to one per - fect whole.
A - gain to lead us for - ward A - long God's ho - ly way.

These words express beautifully the ministry of Jesus, while summoning us to take on his service. List the ways—not worrying about conformity, being courageous, expressing acceptance and kindness to all people—of being open to Jesus' challenge anew.

In the Crowds That Came to Jesus

98

Dorothy Ballard, 1959

IN BABILONE 8.7.8.7.D.
Dutch Melody
Arr. By Julius Röntgen, c. 1906

In the crowds that came to Jesus, Teach-ing up and down the land, There were some who scorned and mocked him, Some who did not un-der-stand. But the ones who lis-tened hum-bly Learned to trust him and o-bey, Learned to love and be for-giv-ing, And be-lieve in Je-sus' way.

99   To Jesus Christ the Children Sang

Alda M. Milner-Barry

ST. COLUMBA 8.7.8.7.
Irish Melody
Harm. by Paul Hamill, 1983

1. To__ Je - sus Christ the__ chil - dren sang Ho - san - na,
2. To__ Je - sus Christ the__ chil - dren sing Ho - san - na,

Lord! Ho - san - na! Through cit - y streets their
Lord! Ho - san - na! With joy - ful hearts our

voic - es rang; Ho - san - na, Lord! Ho - san - na!
praise we bring; Ho - san - na, Lord! Ho - san - na!

100   Jesus Walked This Lonesome Valley

White Spiritual

LONESOME VALLEY Irr.
White Spiritual
Harm. by Paul Hamill, 1983

1. Je - sus walked_____ this lone - some val - ley,_____ He had to
2. You must go_____ and stand your tri - al,_____ You have to

walk___ it by him-self, Oh___ no-bod-y else___ could walk it
stand___ it by your-self, Oh___ no-bod-y else___ can stand it

for him, He had to walk it by___ him-self.
for you, You have to stand it by___ your-self.

O, They Crucified My Lord

101

Black Spiritual

CRUCIFIED LORD Irr.
Black Spiritual
Harm. by Paul Hamill, 1983

Quietly (♩=63), *in unison*

1. O, they cru-ci-fied my Lord, And he nev-er said a mum-ba-lin'
2. O, they nailed him to a tree, And he nev-er said a mum-ba-lin'
3. O, they pierced him in the side, And he nev-er said a mum-ba-lin'
4. O, he bowed his head and died, And he nev-er said a mum-ba-lin'

word: They cru-ci-fied my Lord, And he nev-er said a mum-ba-lin'
word: They nailed him to a tree, And he nev-er said a mum-ba-lin'
word: They pierced him in the side, And he nev-er said a mum-ba-lin'
word: He bowed his head and died, And he nev-er said a mum-ba-lin'

word: Not a word, not a word, not a word.
word: Not a word, not a word, not a word.
word: Not a word, not a word, not a word.
word: Not a word, not a word, not a word.

102

All Glory, Laud, and Honor

Theodulph of Orleans, c. 760–821
Tr. John M. Neale, 1818–1866
Altered, 1983

ST. THEODULPH 7.6.7.6.D.
Melchior Teschner, pub. 1615.

Majestically (♩ =104)

1. All glo - ry, laud and hon - or To you, Re - deem - er, sing,
2. You are the King of Is - rael, And Da - vid's roy - al Son,
3. You did ac - cept their prais - es; Ac - cept the prayers we bring,

To whom the lips of chil - dren Made sweet ho - san - nas ring!
Who in our God's name com - est, The Christ and bless - ed one;
Who in all good de - light - est, O good and gra - cious King.

The peo - ple of the He - brews With palms be - fore you went;
To you, be - fore your pas - sion, They sang their hymns of praise;
All glo - ry, laud, and hon - or To you, Re - deem er, sing,

Our praise and prayer and an - thems Be - fore you we pre - sent.
To you, now high ex - alt - ed, Our mel - o - dy we raise.
To whom the lips of chil - dren Made sweet ho - san - nas ring!

Were You There When They Crucified My Lord

Black Spiritual

WERE YOU THERE Irr.
Black Spiritual
Harm. by Paul Hamill, 1983

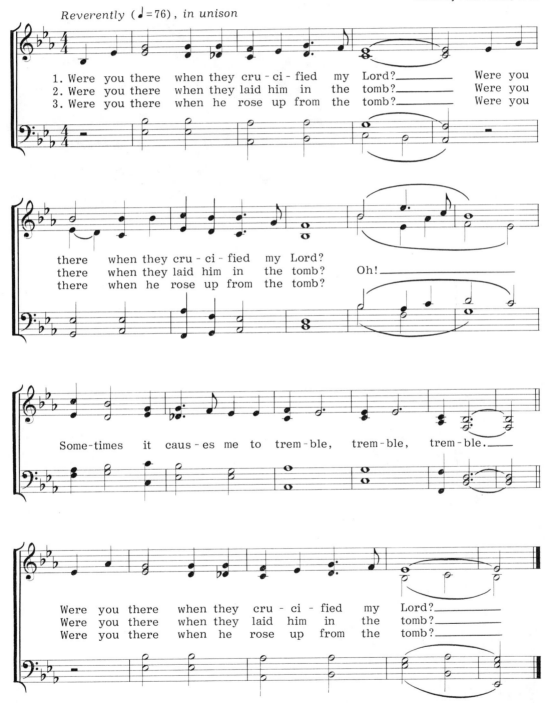

Reverently (♩=76), in unison

1. Were you there when they cru-ci-fied my Lord?_____ Were you
2. Were you there when they laid him in the tomb?_____ Were you
3. Were you there when he rose up from the tomb?_____ Were you

there when they cru-ci-fied my Lord?
there when they laid him in the tomb? Oh!_____
there when he rose up from the tomb?

Some-times it caus-es me to trem-ble, trem-ble, trem-ble._____

Were you there when they cru-ci-fied my Lord?_____
Were you there when they laid him in the tomb?_____
Were you there when he rose up from the tomb?_____

This spiritual expresses the Good Friday sorrow but goes on to speak in awe of the Easter message of Jesus' being raised up from the tomb.

Jesus: Resurrection

As the land is refreshed with Spring, we are inspired and sing our songs of joy at Eastertime. God has raised Jesus Christ in triumph from the dead. This resurrection faith sustains us, as it did Jesus' followers.

Loud Hosannas Let Us Sing

104

Gertrude Priester, 1979

LLANFAIR 7.7.7.7. with Alleluias
Robert Williams, c. 1781–1821
Harm. by David Evans, 1874–1948

With breadth (♩ =100)

1. Loud ho-san-nas let us sing. Al – le-lu – ia!
2. Christ our Lord is here to-day. Al – le-lu – ia!

Wel-come Je-sus Christ the King. Al – le-lu – ia!
Lis-ten now to what we say! Al – le-lu – ia!

You seek Je-sus. Do not fear! Al – le-lu – ia!
Christ our Lord is ris'n to-day! Al – le-lu – ia!

He is ris'n. He is not here. Al – le-lu – ia!
Hear our prais-es as we say Al – le-lu – ia!

105

Jesus Christ Is Ris'n Today

Norman and Margaret Mealy

Medieval Melody

With a lilt (♩.=80), in unison

Je - sus Christ is ris'n to-day, Al - le - lu - ia, Al - le - lu - ia! So

let us all re - joice and say, "Al - le - lu - ia!"

From *Sing for Joy* by Norman and Margaret Mealy. Copyright © 1961 by the Seabury Press, Inc. Used with permission.
May be sung as a two-part round.

106

It Is the Joyful Eastertime

Alda M. Milner-Barry

Traditional Cornish
arr. Norman and Margaret Mealy

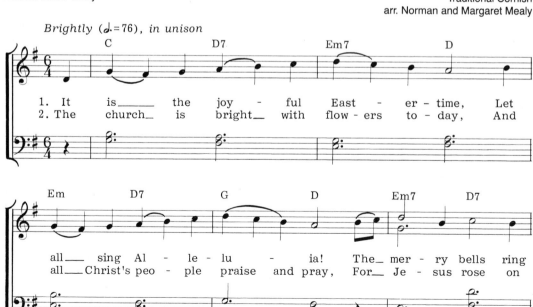

Brightly (♩.=76), in unison

1. It is____ the joy - ful East - er - time, Let
2. The church__ is bright__ with flow - ers to - day, And

all__ sing Al - le - lu - ia! The__ mer - ry bells ring
all__ Christ's peo - ple praise and pray, For__ Je - sus rose on

Joy Dawned Again on Easter Day   107

Latin: 5th Century?
Tr. John M. Neale, 1818–1866, alt.
Adapted by Mary N. Hawkes, 1983

PUER NOBIS L.M.
Adapted by Michael Praetorius, 1609
Harm. by Paul Hamill, 1983

1. Joy dawned a-gain on East-er Day, The sun shone out__ with fair ar-ray. When to their long-ing eyes re-stored, The A-pos-tles saw their ris-en Lord.
2. O God, with Je-sus as our Guide, We pray to keep__ his love a-live; That we may give you all our days, Our will-ing lives in joy-ful praise.
3. O God of all, with us a-bide. In this our joy-ful East-er-tide We pray for strife and wars to cease, Through Je-sus Christ our love and peace.

108   O Sons and Daughters, Let Us Sing

Jean Tisserand, d. 1494
Tr. John M. Neale, 1818–1866, alt.
Adapted by Mary N. Hawkes, 1983

O FILII ET FILIAE 8.8.8. with Alleluias
French Melody, 15th Century

Triumphantly (♩ = 108)

Al - le - lu - ia!___ Al - le - lu - ia! Al - le - lu - ia!

1. O sons and daugh - ters let___ us sing That Je - sus
2. That East - er morn,___ at break___ of day, The faith ful
3. An an - gel spoke___ un - to___ the three And urged them
4. How blessed are they___ who have___ not seen And yet whose
5. On this most hap - py day___ of days, To God your

Christ___ our glo - rious king O'er death to - day___ rose
wom - en went___ their way To seek the tomb___ where
let___ their sor - row flee; "Your Lord is gone___ to
faith___ has con - stant been; In life e - ter - nal
hearts___ and voic - es raise In laud and ju - bi -

tri - umph - ing.
Je - sus lay.
Gal - i - lee."   Al - le - lu - ia!
they___ shall reign.
lee___ and praise.

D.S. %

The words to this folk carol with refrain originally were written by a French Franciscan, Jean Tisserand, in the 15th century. The translation appeared in John Mason Neale's 1851 collection, *Medieval Hymns and Sequences*.

The Strife Is O'er

109

Latin, 17th Century
Tr. Francis Pott, 1832–1909

THE STRIFE IS O'ER 8.8.8. with Alleluias
James Minchin

Steadily (♩=92), in unison
Introduction

Verse

The strife is o'er, the bat-tle done,— Now is the Vic-tor's tri-umph won;— O let the song of praise be sung:—

Chorus

Al-le-lu-ia, Al-le-lu-ia, Al-le-lu-ia, Al-le-lu-ia, Al-le-lu-ia, Al-le-lu-ia, Al-le-lu-ia, Praise the Lord!

Christian Tradition

The biblical tradition—both Old and New Testaments—expresses the hope and wisdom of God in the actions of many persons: patriarchs, kings, prophets, disciples, saints. In these events and personalities, we find inspiration to be followers of the way and saints. We share Jesus' daring dream to change our history and to make our world a better place.

Book of Books, Our People's Strength

Percy Dearmer, 1867–1936
Altered, 1983

LIEBSTER JESU 7.8.7.8.8.8.
Melody by Johann Ahle, 1625–1673
Harm. by J. S. Bach, 1685–1750

110

Moderately slow (♩ =84)

1. Book of__books, our peo-ple's strength, Lead - ers, teach-er's, he - ro's
2. Thank we__those who toiled in thought, Man - y di - verse scrolls com -
3. Praise we__ God, who has in - spired Those whose wis - dom still di -

treas - ure, Bring - ing__ free - dom, spread - ing truth,
plet - ing, Po - ets,__ proph - ets, schol - ars, saints,
rects us; Praise God__ for the Word made flesh,

Shed - ding light that none can meas - ure; Wis - dom comes to
Each with words of God re - peat - ing, Till they came, who
For the Spir - it which pro - tects us. Light of knowl-edge,

those who__ know__ you, All the best we have we owe you.
told the__ sto - ry Of the Word, and showed God's glo - ry.
ev - er__ burn - ing, Shed on us your death - less learn - ing.

111 In Days Before They Counted Time

Mary Duckert, 1973
Adapted, 1979, 1983

Ruth Lowry Sawyers

Narrative 1. In days be-fore they count-ed time When all the world was young, Folk jour-neyed in the Mid-dle East And spoke a sin-gle tongue.___ While in the land of Shi-nar___ They came up-on a plain, And thus be-gan a ven-ture That earned them God's dis-dain.

Bragging 2. "Come, let us build a town," they said, With a tow-er to the sky. We'll man-u-fac-ture bricks for stones___ Reach-ing heav-en by and by. The tow-er will make us might-y.___ The tow-er will bring us fame, While all the world will bow to us And call up-on our name."

Prayerfully 3. When God be-held the build-ers plans, Their han-ker-ing for fame, The mak-er of the worlds cried, "Come, call up-on my name!___ Or I will___ come a-mong you,___ I will con-fuse your speech, Lest an-y-thing you try on earth Will be with-in your reach."

Stanzas 1 and 2

Stanza 3

(chord only)

From *The Teacher's Guide, Revised, Year I*, Grades 5–6. Copyright © MCMLXXI, MCMLXXIII by The Geneva Press. Altered and used by permission.

The events of Pentecost remind Christians that understanding one another comes as we worship together as God's people. The writer of these words, Mary Duckert, is Associate for Children's Resources and Program, Presbyterian Church (U.S.A.).

112   The Bible Tells of God's Great Love

Betty Doughman
Altered, 1983

WINCHESTER OLD C.M.
From Thomas Este's *Whole Book of Psalms,* 1592

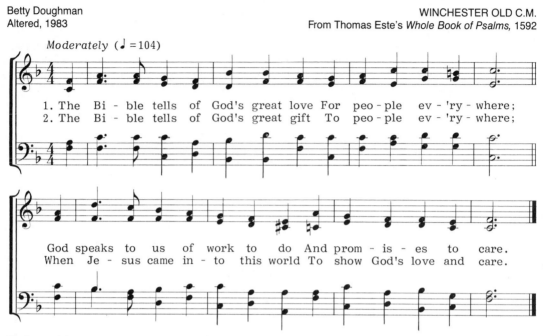

1. The Bi - ble tells of God's great love For peo - ple ev - 'ry - where;
2. The Bi - ble tells of God's great gift To peo - ple ev - 'ry - where;

God speaks to us of work to do And prom - is - es to care.
When Je - sus came in - to this world To show God's love and care.

113   Michael, Row the Boat Ashore

Traditional

Slave Song

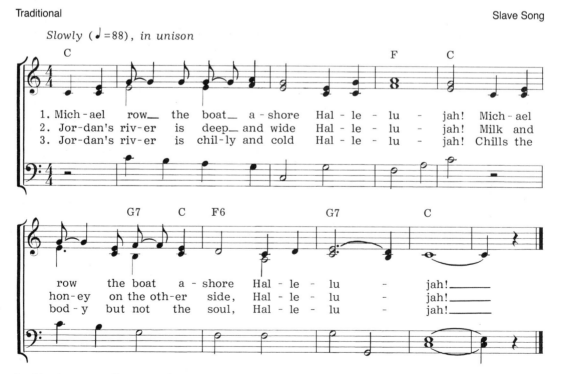

Slowly (♩=88), *in unison*

1. Mich - ael row__ the boat__ a - shore Hal - le - lu - jah! Mich - ael
2. Jor - dan's riv - er is deep__ and wide Hal - le - lu - jah! Milk and
3. Jor - dan's riv - er is chil - ly and cold Hal - le - lu - jah! Chills the

row the boat a - shore Hal - le - lu - jah!____
hon - ey on the oth - er side, Hal - le - lu - jah!____
bod - y but not the soul, Hal - le - lu - jah!____

In this slave song discovered in an 1886 collection by Anthony Saletan, we hear the slave's longing for freedom while at the same time proclaiming the hope found in the tradition.

The Simple Fishermen Cast Nets 114

Edith Lovell Thomas
Altered, 1983

ICH HALTE TREULICH STILL S.M.D.
Johann Sebastian Bach, 1685–1750

Moderately (♩ =96)

1. The sim - ple fish - er - men Cast nets in - to the sea.
2. New trails they broke with him Through fields, up moun - tain - side;
3. They shared his dar - ing dreams: His hope that ev - 'ry one

And Je - sus watched them as he walked Be - side Lake Gal - i - lee;
They cared for sick and hun - gry ones, In train - ing with their Guide.
Would car - ry on, with Je - sus' help, The work he had be - gun.

He called; they rowed a - shore; With joy they made the choice
Com - pan - ions they be - came, Less fear - ful and more brave,
His cir - cle, once so small, Now 'round the earth ex - tends,

To leave their boats for work with him, In - spir - ed by his voice.
And as their love for Je - sus grew, More help to all they gave.
En - larged by those who ven - ture forth To make a world of friends.

115 At the Name of Jesus

Caroline Maria Noel, 1870; alt., 1931

KING'S WESTON 6.5.6.5.D.
Ralph Vaughan Williams, 1872–1958

With vigor (♩=96), *in unison*

1. At the name of Je - sus Ev-'ry knee shall bow,
2. Hum - bled for a sea - son, To re-ceive a name

Ev - 'ry tongue con - fess____ him King of glo - ry now;
From the lips of sin - ners Un - to whom he came,

'Tis__ God's own pleas - ure that We should call him Lord,
Faith - ful - ly he bore_____ it Spot - less to the last,

Who from the be - gin - ning Was the might - y Word.
Brought it back vic - to - rious When from death he passed.

Music from *Enlarged Songs of Praise* by permission of Oxford University Press.

The King of Glory Comes

116

W. F. Jabusch, 1967

PROMISED ONE 12.12.12.12.
Israeli Folk Song
Arr. by John Ferguson, 1973

With increasing tempo (♩ =80 to 126), in unison

Refrain

The King of glo - ry comes, the na - tion re - joic - es.

O - pen the gates be - fore him, lift up your voic - es.

1. Who is the King of glo - ry; how shall we call him?
2. In all of Gal - i - lee, in cit - y or vil - lage,
3. Sing then of Da - vid's Son, our sav - ior and broth - er;
4. He gave his life for us, the pledge of sal - va - tion;
5. He con - quered sin and death; he tru - ly has ris - en.

Repeat Refrain after each stanza

He is Em - man - u - el, the prom - ised of a - ges.
He goes a - mong his peo - ple, cur - ing their ill - ness.
In all of Gal - i - lee was nev - er an - oth - er.
He took up - on him - self the sins of the na - tion.
And he will share with us his heav - en - ly vi - sion.

117 Great Men and Women of the Faith

Mary N. Hawkes, 1983

WELLINGTON SQUARE C.M.D.
Guy Warrack, 1900–?

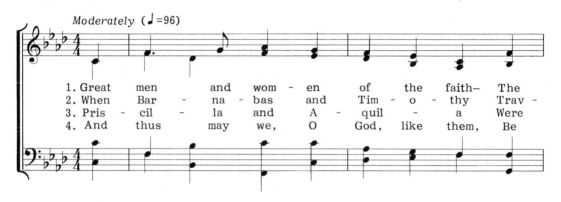

1. Great men and wom - en of the faith— The
2. When Bar - na - bas and Tim - o - thy Trav -
3. Pris - cil - la and A - quil - a Were
4. And thus may we, O God, like them, Be

fol - lowers of the Way Dis - band - ed, sad, at
ersed a - long with Paul, On jour - neys far oe'r
friends of Paul's from Rome, Tent - mak - ers, fol-lowers
fol - lowers of the Way; We ask no price, no

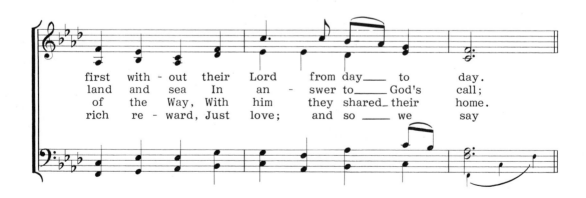

first with - out their Lord from day____ to day.
land and sea In an - swer to____ God's call;
of the Way, With him they shared_ their home.
rich re - ward, Just love; and so ____ we say

Soon	knew	they had	a	task	to	do	To
Kind	Bar - na - bas	the	poor	to	save	His
On	riv - er bank	near	Phil - ip - pi	Paul
That	we	will al - so	fol - low	Christ	And

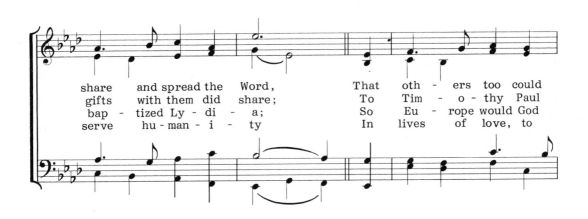

share	and spread the	Word,	That	oth - ers too could
gifts	with them did	share;	To	Tim - o - thy Paul
bap - tized Ly - di - a;	So	Eu - rope would God
serve	hu - man - i - ty	In	lives	of love, to

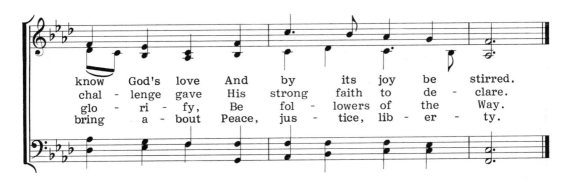

know	God's	love	And	by	its	joy	be	stirred.
chal - lenge	gave	His	strong	faith	to	de - clare.
glo - ri - fy,	Be	fol - lowers of	the	Way.
bring	a - bout	Peace,	jus - tice, lib - er - ty.

The words to this hymn are dedicated to Edna M. Baxter, Professor Emerita of Hartford Seminary, a "great woman of the faith." Mary Hawkes, an editor of SING TO GOD, was influenced by Miss Baxter, as she was student teacher of an 8th Grade Class at Center Church in Hartford.

118 Built on the Rock the Church Does Stand

Nicolai F. S. Grundtvig, 1837
Tr. by Carl Döving, 1909
Altered, 1972, 1979

KIRKEN 8.8.8.8.8.8.8.8.
Ludvig M. Lindeman, 1840

1. Built on the rock the church does stand, E - ven when stee-ples are fall - ing; Crum-bled have spires in ev - 'ry land, Bells still are chim-ing and call - ing; Call-ing the young and old to rest, But a - bove all the soul dis - tressed, Long-ing for rest ev - er - last - ing.

2. Sure - ly in tem - ples made with hands God, the most high is not dwell - ing; High a - bove earth God's tem - ple stands, All earth - ly tem-ples ex - cel - ling; Yet here on earth God's work was done When Je - sus Christ the Cho - sen One Built in our bod - ies his tem - ple.

3. Now we may gath - er with our King, E'en in the low - li - est dwell - ing; Prais - es to him we there may bring, His won-drous mer - cy forth-tell - ing; Je - sus his grace to us ac - cords, Spir - it and life are all his words, His truth does hal - low the tem - ple.

The Church Today

In the church today we work together, praising God and helping one another as the family of God. Through study and love, we find new life while building and serving together as God's church. This church extends around the world in wholeness and unity, each group needing each other group.

119
There's a Church Within Us

Kent Schneider
Altered, 1983

Kent Schneider

Rhythmically (♩ =144), *in unison*

1. There's a church__ with - in us O__ God,__
2. There's po - ten - tial with - in us O__ God,__
3. There's a fire__ with - in us O__ God,__
4. There's some build - ing to be done__ O__ God,__
5. There's the church__ with - in us O__ God,__

There's a church__ with - in us, O__
Some-thing's stir - ring with - in us, O__
A new life's__ a burn - in', O__
There's some build - ing to be done, O__
There's the Church__ with - in us, O__

God.__ Not a build - ing but a
God.__ Some - thing's strain - ing to have
God.__ A__ fire__ for new
God.__ Not with steel,__ not with
God.__ Not a build - ing but one

soul, Not a por - tion but a whole, There's a
birth, To be vis - i - ble on earth, There's po -
life, Com - bat - ting pres - ent strife, There's a
stone, But with lives which are our own, There's the
soul, Not a por - tion but a whole, We__

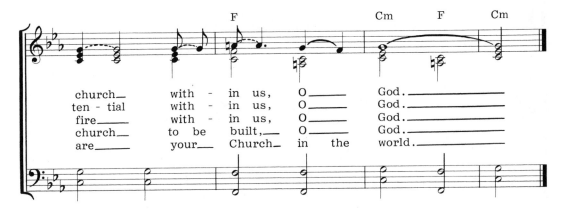

church____ with - in us, O_____ God._____
ten - tial with - in us, O_____ God._____
fire_____ with - in us, O_____ God._____
church____ to be built,___ O_____ God._____
are_____ your___ Church_ in the world._____

Church Bells Ringing

120

Vincent B. Silliman

Melody by Johann Schop, c. 1665
Harm. by Johann Sebastian Bach, 1685–1750 (adapted)

Church bells ring - ing, As they're swing - ing,

Say to peo - ple, "Come__ to - day! Sis - ters, Broth - ers,

Fa - thers, Moth - ers! Meet with friends to__ sing and pray!"

121

The Church Is One Big Family

Margaret C. McNeil

DUNDEE C.M.
Scottish Psalter, 1615

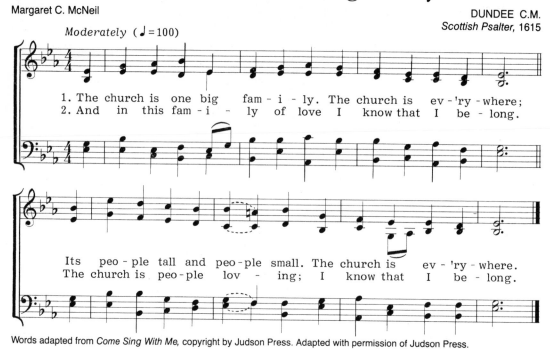

Moderately (♩=100)

1. The church is one big fam - i - ly. The church is ev - 'ry - where;
2. And in this fam - i - ly of love I know that I be - long.

Its peo - ple tall and peo - ple small. The church is ev - 'ry - where.
The church is peo - ple lov - ing; I know that I be - long.

122

We Are Your Church, O God

Elinor Ringland

ST. THOMAS S.M.
Aaron Williams, 1763
New Universal Psalmodist, 1770

Moderately (♩=108)

1. We are your church, O__ God; We__ meet to__ wor - ship you;
2. We are your church, O__ God; We__ meet to__ stud - y, too.
3. We are your church, O__ God, Wher - ev - er__ we may go;

We sing and pray and of - fer gifts And ask what__ may we do.
We learn to share the love you give That oth - ers__ may know you.
We are your peo - ple, serv - ing you, Help us your__ love to show.

This version of the tune, pubished in 1770, was set to Psalm 48. Aaron Williams (1731–1776) was an English music engraver, teacher, and publisher of psalm tune collections.

The Church Is Wherever God's People Are Praising

123

Carol Rose Ikeler, 1959

THE CHURCH Irr.
Vivian Sharp Morsch, 1960

Moderately (♩ =112), *in unison*

1. The church is wher - ev - er God's peo - ple are prais - ing,
2. The church is wher - ev - er God's peo - ple are help - ing,

Sing - ing their thanks_ for__ joy on this day. The
Car - ing for neigh - bors in sick - ness and need. The

church is wher - ev - er dis - ci - ples of Je - sus Re -
church is wher - ev - er God's peo - ple are shar - ing The

mem - ber his sto - ry and walk in his way.
words of the Bi - ble in gift and in deed.

Words and music copyright, 1963, by W. L. Jenkins; from *Songs and Hymns for Primary Children.* Used by permission of The Westminster Press.

124 A Ship That Calls Itself the Church

Martin G. Schneider
Tr. Mary N. Hawkes, 1983

Martin G. Schneider

Boldly (♩ = 96), *in unison*

1. A___ ship that calls it - self the Church,___ The voyage of time its
2. That___ ship that calls it - self the Church,___ Oft lies in har - bor
3. In the ship that calls it - self the Church,___ Each du - ty's glad - ly

sea, Knows where to go be - cause its aim___ Is God's e - ter - ni-
fast, Be - cause life is more com - fort - able___ While look - ing to the
done, Or each one goes a dif - f'rent way___ And feels lost and a-

ty. The ship moves on with threats of storm Through dan - ger, risk, and
past. But if we risk and dan - ger fear, We lose our sight of
lone. When each one glad - ly does a job, And each works with the

fear, De - spair, hope, strug - gle, vic - to - ry; It
God, Who in the wise but qui - et voice, Will
whole, The fear and lone - li - ness dis - solve, As

trav - els year on year.   And still a - gain one
be our strength and guide.   On - ly if we take
each per - forms a role.   And so we trav - el

asks one - self;__ Will it be - calmed re - main,   Or
ven - tures on__ Will we our goal at - tain: To
far and wide__ On this trip through the sea,   With

per - ish in the rest-less sea,__ Its goal not to at - tain?
live in peace and fu - ture hope__ With God's own love our aim.
friends we love and serve and act__ In true com - mu - ni - ty.

O stay by us,__ God; O__ stay by us,__ God; Or__

else we're a-lone on the trip through the sea, O stay by us, God.

Text and Mel.: Martin G. Schneider; Text engl.: Mary N. Hawkes; © Gustav Bosse Verlag Regensburg.

The young people of Heilandskirche in West Berlin loved this hymn, which brings us a message of the need for the ecumenical church. Mary Hawkes, translator of these words and Secretary for Educational Programs for the United Church Board for Homeland Ministries, worked with these young people in the late 1960s.

Community

In community, we are aware of our differences, but we accept all persons who are one in the sharing of gifts. We find God's presence in relationships as we celebrate and minister in community, rooted in love and finding God's light and peace in our neighbors. We share food and shelter with sisters and brothers as we work together for the good of all.

125 # How Good It Is and How Pleasant

Paraphrase of Psalms 133:1
Altered, 1983

PEOPLE TO DWELL TOGETHER Irr.
Jewish Folk Song

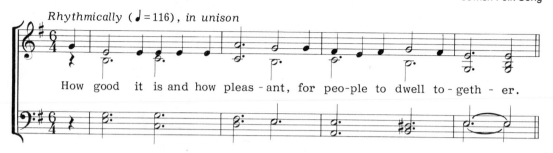

How good it is and how pleas-ant, for peo-ple to dwell to-geth-er.

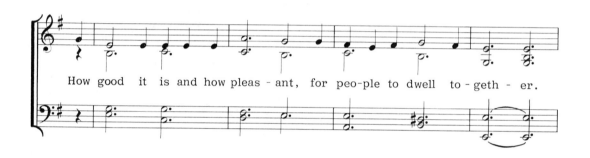

How good it is and how pleas-ant, for peo-ple to dwell to-geth-er.

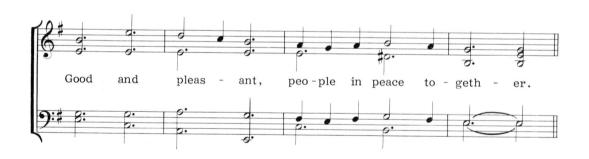

Good and pleas-ant, peo-ple in peace to-geth-er.

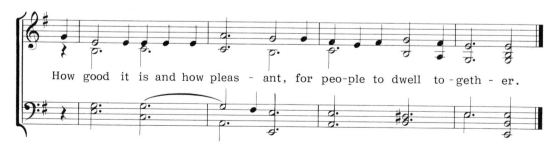

How good it is and how pleas-ant, for peo-ple to dwell to-geth-er.

O Christian, Love Your Sister and Your Brother

126

Ephesians 4:31–32, 5:1–2
John Greenleaf Whittier, 1846, alt.
Adapted by Ruth Duck, 1981

WELWYN 11.10.11.10.
Alfred Scott-Gatty, 1847–1918

Moderately (♩ = 112)

1. O Chris - tian, love your sis - ter and your broth - er:
2. Fol - low with rev - 'rent steps the great ex - am - ple
3. Then shall all shack - les fall: the storm - y clan - gor

Where pit - y dwells, the peace of God is there.
Of Je - sus whose sole work was do - ing good;
Of wild war mu - sic o'er the earth shall cease.

To wor - ship right - ly is to love each oth - er,
So shall the wide earth seem a hal - low'd tem - ple,
Love shall tread out the bale - ful fire of an - ger,

Each smile a hymn, each kind - ly deed a prayer.
Each lov - ing life a hymn of grat - i - tude.
And in its ash - es plant the tree of peace.

127 God of Our Life, of All That We Encounter

Mary N. Hawkes, 1966
Adapted, 1983

ISTE CONFESSOR (ROUEN) 11.11.11.5.
Poitiers Antiphoner, 1746

Moderately (♩ = 116)

1. God of our life, of all that we en - coun - ter,
2. We know that of - ten we must learn through strug - gles,
3. In fam - 'ly liv - ing, day to day with neigh - bor,
4. For this, our Church, we pray with deep sin - cer - i - ty,

We thank you now for all you love and give to us;
Through strife and strain we grow and learn a - bout our-selves;
We need to know that you are al - ways with us;
That it may ev - er see new ways of min - is - try,

For food and home and all our dai - ly
We find it so hard to love our neigh - bor
In each re - la - tion - ship, we may see your
To those who live in ru - ral place or

sus - te - nance, Thank you, O God of Life.
as our - selves; Teach us, O God of Growth.
pres - ence; Guide us, O Nur - tur - er.
cit - y; Help us, O God of Love.

The words to this hymn are dedicated to Jessie N. and William E. Hawkes.

How Beautiful the Springtime Is

128

Lois Horton Young

SHEPHERDS' PIPES C.M.D.
Annabeth McClelland Gay, 1925

In moderate time (♩=104)

1. How beau - ti - ful the spring-time__ is With ear - ly child-hood's glow,
2. The sum-mer-time of youth un - folds With fer - vor and with heat.
3. The bril-liance of the au - tumn__comes With whirl-ing winds a - pace.
4. But win - ter has its beau - ty__ too, Rich full-ness it can bring,

With vig - or fresh and won - der - ment As day by__ day we grow,
New dreams and yearn-ings fill our__hearts, Our hopes and__strength are sweet.
Life's great de - mands up - on us__ fall With ques-tions__ giv - ing chase.
Much wis - dom, judg-ment, joy and__ hope, And now we__ glad - ly sing

With loved ones, treas-ures, play, and__ time A great new world__ to__ know.
The wid'n - ing world in - vites the__steps Of ea - ger climb - ing__ feet.
Each brim-ming day has its re - wards, A man - y splen-dored face.
With cer - tain - ty that there will__come An e - ven love - lier__spring.

O God of years, for child - hood__ days We sing to__ you our praise.
O God of years, for youth's swift__ days We sing to__ you our praise.
O God of mid - dle years, these__ days Lead us to__ sing your praise.
O God of years, for these great__ days We sing to__ you our praise.

Springtime, Summertime, Autumn, Winter—all are part of the natural world as all the ages are part of human life. We may move about among these times. Sometimes we feel like Springtime, sometimes like Winter, but all are needed to keep balance and order.

129 God of Change and Glory

Al Carmines

Al Carmines

With spirit (♩=72), *in unison*

1. God of change and glo - ry, God of time and space,
When we fear the fu - ture Give to us Your grace.
In the midst of chang-ing ways Give us still the grace to praise.

2. God of man - y col - ors, God of man - y signs,
You have made us dif - f'rent, Bless - ings man - y kinds.
As the old ways dis - ap - pear Let Your love cast out our fear.

3. Fresh-ness of the morn - ing, New - ness of each night,
You are still cre - at - ing End - less love and light.
This we see, as shad-ows part, Man - y gifts from one great heart.

Man - y gifts, one Spir - it, One love known in man - y ways.

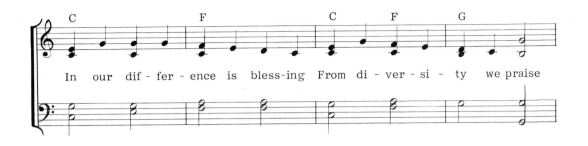

In our dif-fer-ence is bless-ing From di-ver-si-ty we praise

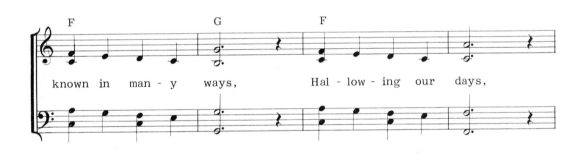

One Giv-er, one Lord, one Spir-it, One Word

known in man-y ways, Hal-low-ing our days,

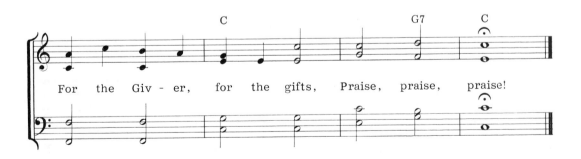

For the Giv-er, for the gifts, Praise, praise, praise!

130   There Is Love All Around You

Betty White
Altered, 1983

LOVE Irr.
Betty White

Gently (♩=96), *in unison*

1. There is   love   all a - round you,   There is
2. There is   peace   if we seek it,   There is
3. There are tears   all a - round you,   There are
4. Like a   stream   grow-ing strong - er,   Love is

joy   on the wind.   Stretch your hand   to your
truth   that will win.   There is God   in our
souls   with - out friend.   Feel the pain   of an -
shared   friend to friend   And flows on   to the

broth - er,   And new life   will be -
sis - ter;   God is love —   let love
oth - er,   And let love   bloom a -
Mak - er,   Love is life   with - out

gin. Stretch your hand to your
in. There is God in our
gain! Feel the pain of an -
end. Love flows on to the

sis - ter, And new life will be - gin!
broth - er; God is love — let love in!
oth - er, And let love bloom a - gain!
Mak - er, Love is life with-out end!

131   We Want to Learn to Live in Love

Dosia Carlson, 1965

CANONBURY L.M.
Arr. from Robert Schumann, 1810–1846

1. We want to learn to__ live in__ love: To fol-low what is
2. When we are sad or__ feel ing__mean And fail to love or
3. When oth-ers are un-kind to__ us And make us want to

good and true. Through friends at church, at__ home, at__ play,
to be fair. Our friends at church, at__ home, at__ play,
cry or fight. We can reach out to__ be good_friends,

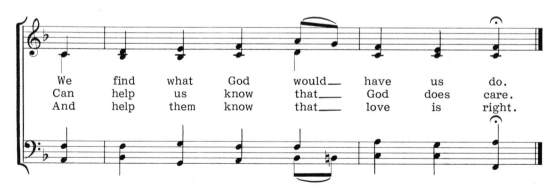

We find what God would__ have us do.
Can help us know that__ God does care.
And help them know that__ love is right.

We Thank You, God, for Strength of Arm 132

Robert Davis, 1908
Altered, 1972, 1983

O JESU 8.6.8.6.8.8.8.
Melody Attr. to Johann Reimann
Hirschberg Gesangbuch, 1741

Deliberately (♩=104)

1. We thank you, God, for strength of arm
2. We thank you, God, for shel - tered home
3. We thank you, God, for lav - ish love

To win our bread, And that, be - yond our need, is meat
In cold and storm, And that, be - yond our need, is room
On us be - stowed, E - nough to share with love - less folk

For friends un - fed: We thank you much for
For friends for - lorn: We thank you much for
To ease their load: Your love to us we

bread to live; We thank you more for bread to give.
place to rest, But more for shel - ter for our guest.
ill could spare, Yet dear - er is your love we share.

133   It Makes No Difference Who We Are

Doris Clare Demaree
Adapted by Mary N. Hawkes, 1983

LOBT GOTT IHR CHRISTEN 8.6.8.8.6.
Melody by Nicolaus Hermann, c. 1485–1561
Harm. by Johann Sebastian Bach, 1685–1750

1. It makes no dif - f'rence who we___ are, What
2. It makes no dif - f'rence where we___ live, In

lan - guage we may speak; What mat - ters are the___
cit - y, town, or farm. God loves us well and___

things we___ do, And how we treat our
hears our___ prayers; God knows our needs, our

neigh - bors___ too, The choic - es___ that we make.
hopes, our___ cares, And helps us___ be our best.

Up, My Neighbor, Come Away

134

Steuart Wilson

LEVEZ-VOUS, MON VOISIN 7.7.8.8. with Refrain
French Melody
Arr. by Martin Shaw, 1875–1958

1. Up, my neigh-bor, come a - way, See the work for us to-day, The hands to help, the mouths to feed, The sights to see, the books to read: Up and get us gone, to help the world a - long, Up and get us gone, my neigh-bor.

2. Up, my neigh-bor, let us pray, Thank our Mak-er ev-'ry day, Who gives us work our strength to test And makes us glad to do our best: Up and get us gone, to help the world a - long, Up and get us gone, my neigh-bor.

135   'Tis the Gift to Be Simple

Traditional

SIMPLE GIFTS Irr.
Shaker Song
Harm. by Paul Hamill, 1983

This is by far the best-known of the thousands of Shaker songs. The imagery expressed in Shaker songs is often biblical and pastoral. Renunciation of the self is made in the vow not to stand stiff with pride like a stubborn oak, but to wave and bow and bend like the willow in the wind of God's will. The Shaker communal sòcietỳ demonstrated the vitality that worship and music can bring to movement. A simple dance could be done to this song.

Ring Out the Old, Ring in the New
136

Alfred Tennyson, 1847
Altered, 1983

DEUS TUORUM MILITUM L.M.
Grenoble Church Melody

1. Ring out the old, ring in the new; Ring, happy bells, across the snow; The year is going, let it go; Ring out the false; ring in the true.

2. Ring out a slowly dying cause; And ancient forms of party strife; Ring in the nobler modes of life, With sweeter manners, purer laws.

3. Ring out old shapes of foul disease; Ring out the narrowing lust of gold; Ring out the thousand wars of old; Ring in the thousand years of peace.

137 We Have This Ministry

Jim Strathdee   Jim Strathdee

Moderately (♩ =96), *in unison*

1. We have this min - is - try, And we are not dis-
2. O Christ, the tree of life, Our end and our be-
3. The yoke of Christ is ours, The whole world is our

cour - aged. It is by God's own pow'r That
gin - ning, We grow to full - est flow'r When
par - ish, We dai - ly take the cross, The

we may live and serve. O - pen - ly we share God's word,
rest - ed in your love. Broth - ers, sis - ters, cler - gy, lay,
bur - den, and the joy. Bear - ing hurts of those we serve,

Speak - ing truth as we be - lieve, Pray - ing that the
Called to serv - ice by your grace, Dif - f'rent cul - tures,
Wound - ed, bruised, and bowed with pain, Ho - ly Spir - it,

shad - owed world May heal - ing light re - ceive. We
dif - f'rent gifts, The young and old a place. We
bread and wine, We die and rise a - gain. We

have this min - is - try, O God, re-ceive our liv - ing.
have this min - is - try, O God, re-ceive our giv - ing.
have this min - is - try, O God, re-ceive our lov - ing.

138   I Am the Light of the World

Howard Thurman and
Jim Strathdee, 1969

Jim Strathdee

Moderately (♩ = 100), *in unison*

"I am the light of the world!

You peo - ple come and fol - low me!"   If you

fol - low   and   love   You'll learn the mys - ter - y   Of

what   you were meant to do and   be._____

Discipleship and Mission

Our love and service go outside of our own church and community to the world around us and beyond, to towns and cities, to areas of need. As followers of Jesus, we covenant to live our faith and teach others to live by God's commandments. We share the good news, united in love and service to the poor, the friendless, the ill, and suffering persons wherever they may be.

Awake, Awake, to Love and Work

139

Geoffrey A. Studdert-Kennedy, 1883–1929
Altered by Mary N. Hawkes, 1983

MORNING SONG 8.6.8.6.8.6.
Melody, *Kentucky Harmony,* 1816
Harm. by C. Winfred Douglas, 1867–1944

With a lilt (♩=120)

1. A - wake, a wake to_ love and_ work! The lark is in the
2. Come, let your voice be_ one with_theirs, Shout with their shout of
3. To give and give, and_ give a - gain, What God's giv'n you and

sky; The_ fields are_ wet with dia - mond_ dew; The
praise; See how the_ gi - ant sun soars_ up, Great
me; To_ spend our - selves nor count the_ cost; To

worlds a - wake_ to cry Their_ bless - ings_ on the
God of years_ and days! So_ let the_ love of
serve right glo - rious - ly The_ God who_ gave all

Lord of_ life, As he goes meek - ly by.
Je - sus_ come And set your soul a - blaze.
worlds that_ are, And all that are_ to be.

140   I Sing a Song of the Saints Today

Mary Duckert, 1974
Altered, 1979

WOODMERE, Irr.
Paul Hamill, 1974

they re - fuse. But they're all of them saints___ of
hope it's in me. So I'll join the___ peo - ple who

God, and___ we, God help - ing, can be saints___ too.
love and in-tend, God help - ing, to be saints___ too.

The word "saints" in the New Testament refers to all the followers of Jesus, not just those honored after their death for extraordinary deeds. The same may be said today.

Love God With All Your Soul and Strength   141

Mark 12:30–31
Adapted by Isaac Watts, 1715

FARRANT Irr.
From John Hilton, c. 1560–1608

Quietly (♩=96), in unison

Love God with all your soul and strength, With

all___ your heart and mind; Love your neigh - bor

as your - self,___ Be faith - ful, just, and kind.

142 Jesus, Our Lord, Was Friend to All

Lyn Beckwith, 1963
Altered, 1983

TALLIS' CANON L.M.
Thomas Tallis, c. 1567

1. Je - sus, our Lord, was friend to all, And
2. His teach - ings speak to guide us still In

in our hearts we hear his call To love and serve, and
all our lives to do God's will, Like him, we seek God's

seek to be A friend in word and deed, as he.
help in prayer And trust God's con - stant, lov - ing care.

Words copyright 1963, United Church Press.

*The canon begins here. See note for 9, "Our Thanks to You, O God," for further information.

143 When Jesus Saw the Fishermen

Edith Agnew, 1953

ST. STEPHEN 8.6.8.6.
William Jones, 1789

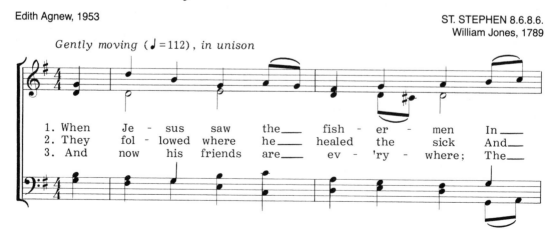

1. When Je - sus saw the___ fish - er - men In___
2. They fol - lowed where he___ healed the sick And___
3. And now his friends are___ ev - 'ry - where; The___

boats up - on the sea, He called to them, "Come,
gave the_ hun - gry bread, And oth - ers joined them
cir - cle_ once so small Ex - tends a - round the

leave your_ nets And fol - low,_ fol - low me."
as they_ went Wher - ev - er_ Je - sus led.
whole wide_ world, For Je - sus_ calls us all.

Help Us, O God, to Learn 144

William W. Reid, Jr.

SCHUMANN S.M.
Cantica Laudis, 1850
Arr. from Robert Schumann, 1810–1856

Moderately fast (♩ =116)

1. Help us, O God to learn The truths your word im - parts;_ To
2. Help us, O God to live The faith which we pro - claim,_ That
3. Help us, O God to teach The mean - ing of your ways,_ That

stud - y that your laws may be In - scribed up-on our hearts.
all our thoughts and words and deeds May glo - ri - fy your name.
search-ing ones may learn of Christ And sing a - loud your praise.

145 You Shall Love the Lord Your God

Matthew 22:37, 39

Paul Hamill, 1983

1. You shall love the Lord your God with all your heart, with
2. You shall love your neigh - bor, your neigh-bor as your-

all your soul, with all your mind.
self, your neigh - bor as your - self.

You shall love the Lord your God.
You shall love the Lord your God.

146 Wherever People Live in Love

Dorothy B. Fritz, 1959

LOBT GOTT IHR CHRISTEN 8.6.8.6.6.
Nicolaus Hermann, c. 1485–1561
Harm. by Johann Sebastian Bach, 1685–1750

Wher - ev - er peo - ple live in love, And wor - ship, sing, and

pray As fol - low - ers of Je - sus Christ, These

are the Peo - ple of__ the__ Way, The Peo - ple__ of the Way.

Your Work, O God, Needs Many Hands 147

Calvin W. Laufer, 1874–1938, alt.

AMAZING GRACE C.M.
American Folk Hymn
Virginia Harmony, 1831

With spirit (♩ =96), in unison

1. Your work, O__ God, needs man - y hands To
2. Be - cause we__ love you and your work, Our

help you__ ev - 'ry - where; And some__ there__ are who
of - f'ring__ now we make; Be pleased__ to__ use it

can - not__ serve Un - less our__ gifts we share.
as__ your__ own, We ask for__ Je - sus' sake.

After the publication of this tune in the *Virginia Harmony*, it gained great popularity through its appearance in the *Southern Harmony* in 1835. It is effective to hum through the complete melody with a unison accompaniment and then sing the two verses.

148 Jesu, Jesu, Fill Us With Your Love

John 13:3–5
From Ghana
Tr. by Tom Colvin

CHEREPONI Irr.
Ghana Melody
Arr. by Jane M. Marshall, 1981

In a gentle two (♩.=63), in unison

Je - su,_____ Je - su,_____ fill us with your love, show

us how to serve the neigh-bors we have from you.

1. Kneels at the feet of his friends, si - lent-ly wash-es their
2. Neigh-bors are rich__ and poor, neigh-bors are black__ and
3. These are the ones we should serve, these are the ones we should
4. Lov - ing puts us on our knees, serv - ing as though we are
5. Kneel at the feet of our friends, si - lent-ly wash-ing their

feet, Mas - ter who acts as a slave__ to them.
white, neigh-bors are near__ and far__ a - way.
love. All__ are neigh-bors to us__ and you.
slaves, this is the way we should live__ with you.
feet, this is the way we should live__ with you.

This gentle song from Ghana helps us to consider the servant role of Jesus as recorded in John 13, a role that we, too, may assume.

I Have Heard Good News Today

149

Abraham Mumol, alt.
Tr. by George R. Flora

Buzi People Melody
From the Reverend George R. Flora

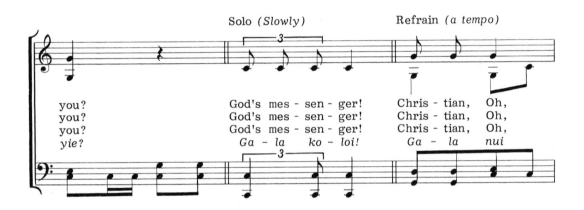

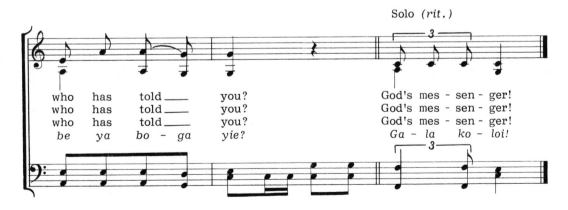

This African song expresses the importance of witnessing to our faith.

150 Heart and Mind, Possessions, God

Narayan V. Tilka, 1862–1919
Tr. Alden H. Clark and Others
Altered, 1983

TANA MANA DHANA (Marathi) Irr.
Ancient Indian Melody
Adapted by Marion Jean Chute

Freely (♩=80)

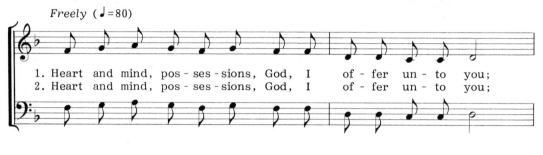

1. Heart and mind, pos - ses - sions, God, I of - fer un - to you;
2. Heart and mind, pos - ses - sions, God, I of - fer un - to you;

All these were yours, God; You gave them all to me.
You are the Way, the Truth; you are the Life.

Won - drous are your do - ings un - to me. Plans and my thoughts and
Sin - ful, I com - mit my - self to you. Je - sus Christ is fill - ing

ev - 'ry - thing I ev - er do are de - pend - ent on your
all the heart of me. He can give me vic - tory o'er

will and love a - lone. I com - mit my spir - it un - to you.
all that threat - ens me. Je - sus Christ is fill - ing all my heart.

Come, Let Us Now Lift Up Our Voices   151

Doris M. Gill

FOUNDATION 11.11.11.11.
William Caldwell's *Union Harmony,* 1837

Moderately (♩=96), *in unison*

1. Come, let us now lift up our voic - es in praise, And to the Cre - a - tor a thanks - giv - ing raise, For towns with their build - ings of stone, steel, and wood, For peo - ple who love them and work for their good.

2. We thank you, O God, for the num - ber-less things And friends and ad - ven - tures which ev - 'ry day brings. O may we not rest un - til all that we view In towns and in cit - ies is pleas - ing to you.

152 The Light of God Is Falling

Louis F. Benson, 1910
Adapted by Mary Duckert, 1979

AURELIA 7.6.7.6.D
Samuel Sebastian Wesley, 1810–1876

Quietly (♩ =96)

The light of God is fall - ing Up - on life's com -mon way;

Hear Je - sus' voice still call - ing, "Come, walk with me to - day";

Re - mem - ber his com - pas - sion, Un - self - ish love for all.

As we love in this fash - ion, We an - swer Je - sus' call.

United in the Love of God

Frank von Christierson, 1961
Altered, 1983

ELLACOMBE 7.6.7.6.D.
Gesangbuch Wirtemberg, 1784

Moving along (♩=116), *in unison*

1. U - nit - ed____ in the love of God, We serve__ God's chil - dren here,
2. O you whose__ love en-folds us all, Whose wis - dom is our might,
3. Take from our__ hearts all greed and hate, All self - ish thought and aim,

The poor, the__ sick, the friend-less folk Weighed down__ by doubt and fear.
Show us the__ way to help and heal, To give__ and serve a - right;
That we may__ give our-selves in love As those__ who hear the name

We__ see them through the eyes of__ Christ, Be - wil-dered and dis-tressed,
Make__ us the a - gents of your__ peace, The__ bear-ers of your light,
Of__ Je - sus Christ the cru - ci - fied, Who__ loved us to the end

De - fi - ant__ youth and hope-less souls, By count - less woes op-pressed.
The means by__ which your love is known How-ev - er dark the night.
And gave him - self in love for all, The world's__ e - ter - nal friend.

154   We Covenant With Hand and Heart

Samuel T. Benade, 1746–1830 (1792)
Adapted by Mary N. Hawkes, 1983

DER SABBATH IST UNS MENSCHEN WILL'N 8.6.8.6.8.8.6.
C. Gregor *Choralbuch,* 1784

We cov-e-nant with hand and heart To fol-low—Christ, our Lord; De-part-ing from self-cen-tered-ness and liv-ing— by God's word. To love each oth-er heart-i-ly In truth and with sin-cer-i-ty, And through all thoughts and acts— al-ways To glo-ri-fy God's Name.

The covenant, both in the Old Testament and in the New Testament, demands of us a loyalty and a commitment to those in our community and to God. We expect the same in return.

God's Global Family

As we go outward from the church to the world, we share the dream to be one family of God. We dream dreams; we share visions; we pray that we all may be one in Christ. Although we are different, inside we are alike, as all humankind unites in love and service.

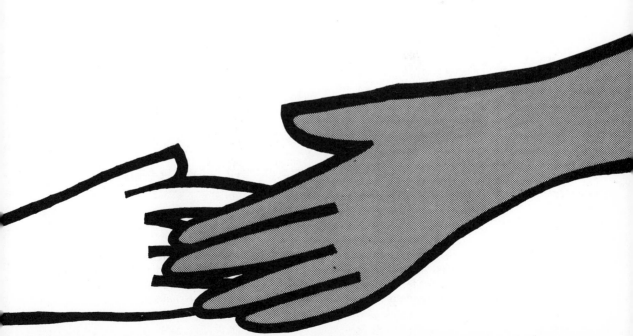

155 We All Are One in Jesus Christ

Mary N. Hawkes, 1984

McKEE C.M.
Black Melody
Adapted by Harry T. Burleigh, 1866–1949

Brightly (♩=100)

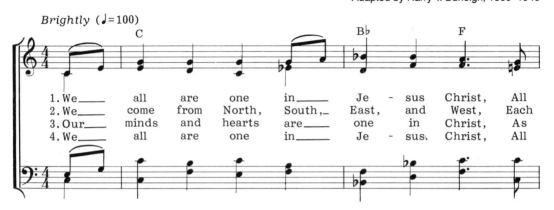

1. We___ all are one in___ Je - sus Christ, All
2. We___ come from North, South,_ East, and West, Each
3. Our___ minds and hearts are___ one in Christ, As
4. We___ all are one in___ Je - sus, Christ, All

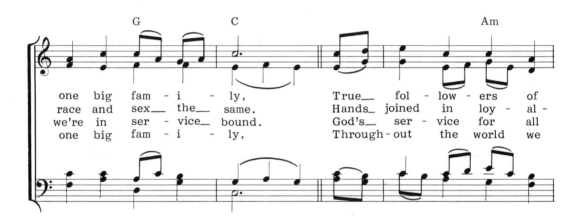

one big fam - i - ly, True__ fol - low - ers of
race and sex__ the__ same. Hands__ joined in loy - al -
we're in ser - vice__ bound. God's__ ser - vice for all
one big fam - i - ly, Through - out the world we

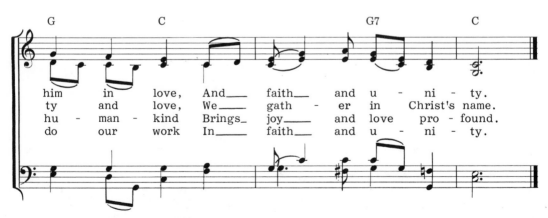

him in love, And__ faith__ and u - ni - ty.
ty and love, We__ gath - er in Christ's name.
hu - man - kind Brings_ joy__ and love pro - found.
do our work In__ faith__ and u - ni - ty.

These words are written in honor of Martin Luther King, Jr. Harry T. Burleigh (1866–1949), the grandson of a slave, arranger of this melody, wrote,

The plantation songs known as "spirituals" are the spontaneous outbursts of intense religious fervor, and had their origin chiefly in camp meetings, revivals and other religious exercises. They were never 'composed,' but sprang into life, ready made, from the white heat of religious fervor . . . as the simple, ecstatic utterance of wholly untutored minds. (From *Guide to the Pilgrim Hymnal.*)

We, God's People, Praise

156

Kate Stearns Page, 1873–1963
Adapted by Mary N. Hawkes, 1983

ST. ANTHONY'S CHORALE Irr.
Franz Joseph Haydn, 1732–1809
Arr. from Brahms' Variations

Majestically (♩=96), in unison

1. We, God's peo-ple, praise,— praise the God of ev-'ry na-tion!
2. We, God's peo-ple, praise,— praise the God of ev-'ry na-tion!

We, God's peo-ple, praise,— praise the God of hosts e-ter-nal!
We, God's peo-ple, praise,— praise the God of hosts e-ter-nal!

Days of won-der, days of beau-ty, Days of rap-ture, filled with light;
For rich bless-ings, for rich boun-ty, Joy-ful songs to God we sing,

Tell of good-ness, tell of mer-cies, Tell of glo-rious might.—
Songs of glo-ry, songs of tri-umph, To our God we bring.—

We, God's peo-ple, praise,— praise,— Praise God ev-er-more!
We, God's peo-ple, praise,— praise,— Praise God ev-er-more!

157   We Thank You for our Friends

Beatrice J. Vetrano, 1959, alt.

H. Hartsough, 1828–1919
Harm. by M. E. H.

Simply (♩=108), in unison

1. We___ thank you for our friends, for those with whom we play.
2. We___ pray, dear God, for all the friends we do not know,

We ask that you will care for them, dear God, through ev-'ry day.
That boys and girls of ev-'ry land, may know your love al - so.

158   Have We Not All One Loving God

Elizabeth W. Gale

OLD HUNDREDTH L.M.
Louis Bourgeois, c. 1510–1561
Genevan Psalter, 1551

With dignity (♩=92)

Have we not all one lov - ing God? Has

not one God cre - a - ted us? To one big fam - 'ly

we be - long; O let us praise God with our song!

We Are the Cared About People

159

Dosia Carlson, 1971

Dosia Carlson, 1971

Moderately (♩. = 66), *in unison*

1. We are the cared a-bout peo - ple, Cared for in won-drous ways,___
2. We are the cared a-bout peo - ple, Spir - it filled, more than beast,___
3. We are the cared a-bout peo - ple So we may spread that care;___

Mir - a - cle born of each morn-ing, Sun-light to strength-en our days.___
Of - ten re-bel-lious and ug - ly, Yet each can be___ a priest.___
Sens-ing the joy and frus - tra - tion Of those whose lives___ we share.___

Thank God who cares a-bout peo - ple, Hair - y or freck-led, or
Thank God who cares a-bout peo - ple, Teeth - ing or sag-ging with
Thank God who cares a-bout peo - ple, Trust - ing that we will re-

bald,___ We are God's one hu - man fam - 'ly,
years,___ We are God's one hu - man fam - 'ly,
turn___ Love to God's one hu - man fam - 'ly,

Sis - ters and broth - ers we're called, Sis - ters and broth - ers we're called.
Loved just the way each ap - pears, Loved just the way each ap - pears.
Love we re - ceive, nev - er earn, Love we re - ceive, nev - er earn.

160 O People, Come, and Raise Your Voice

Jim Strathdee, 1979
Altered, 1979, 1983

Hebrew Melody
Jim Strathdee, alt. 1979

Moderately fast (♩=116), in unison

Oh peo-ple, come and_ raise your_ voice; Sing our_ song to-geth-er.

Joy shall come to_ this strange_ land When we_ love each oth-er. The_

old shall dream_ new_ dreams. And the young shall_ see a might-y

vi-sion: In the day that God_ has_ made We will end our_ hate-ful di-

vi - sion. Oh_ joy shall come to the cit-y street When our

This Israeli melody has been used by the writer to express a hymn of love and peace, proclaiming that we live together in harmony. A group might enjoy dancing to this song.

161 We Love Because God First Loved Us

Mary Duckert

ECHO SONG Irr.

Peace and Justice

Through the Exodus, Israel found its freedom from bondage and its vision in the land of promise. Our hope is that through Shalom, freedom from bondage is found in a land where justice dominates and hunger disappears. We pray for wars to cease in our time. We are called to be peacemakers—channels of God's peace—who live in faith, hope, joy, unafraid in the love we find in the cross of Christ.

162
Lead On, O Cloud of Presence

Ruth Duck, 1974

LANCASHIRE 7.6.7.6.D.
Henry Smart, 1836

In moderate time (♩ = 108)

1. Lead on, O cloud of Pres - ence, The ex - o - dus is come;
2. Lead on, O fi - ery pil - lar: We fol - low, yet with fears;
3. Lead on, O God of free - dom, Our guid - ing spir - it be,

In wil - der - ness and des - ert Our tribe shall make its home.
But we shall come re - joic - ing, Though joy be born of tears.
Though those who start the jour - ney The prom - ise may not see.

Our slav - ery left be - hind us, A vi - sion in us grows:
We are not lost though wan - der - ing, For by your light we come,
We pray our sons and daugh - ters May live to see that land

We seek the land of prom - ise, Where milk and hon - ey flows.
And we are still God's peo - ple; The jour - ney is our home.
Where jus - tice rules with mer - cy, And love is law's de - mand.

"Lancashire" was first published in the English Presbyterian hymnbook, *Psalms and Hymns for Divine Worship,* 1867.

When Israel Was in Egypt's Land 163

Black Spiritual

GO DOWN MOSES Irr.
Black Spiritual

Freely (♩ =100), in unison

1. When Is - rael was in E - gypt's land,
2. Thus saith the Lord, bold Mo - ses said, Let my peo-ple go,
3. No more in bond - age shall they toil,

Op-pressed so hard they could not stand,
If not I'll smite your first-born dead, Let my peo-ple go.
Let them come out with E-gypt's spoil,

Refrain - in harmony

Go down, Mo - ses, 'Way down in E-gypt's land, ___

Tell_ old ___ Pha - raoh, ___ To let my peo-ple go.

The style of many spirituals suggests that certain phrases (marked I) be sung by a soloist or small group, with the congregation responding (II).

164 And People All 'Neath Their Vines

From Micah 4:3–4, Isaiah 2:4
Paraphrase by Fran Minkoff and Leah Jaffa
Adapted, 1983

Traditional Hebrew
Harm. by M. E. H.

In moderate time (♩=100), in unison

And peo-ple all 'neath their vines and fig trees shall live in

peace and un-a-fraid; 1. And peo-ple fraid; 2.

And in-to plow-shares turn their swords; na-tions shall learn war no more.

165 Shalom Chaverim

Traditional

SHALOM CHAVERIM
Israeli Round Irr.

Rhythmically (♩=104), in unison

Dm

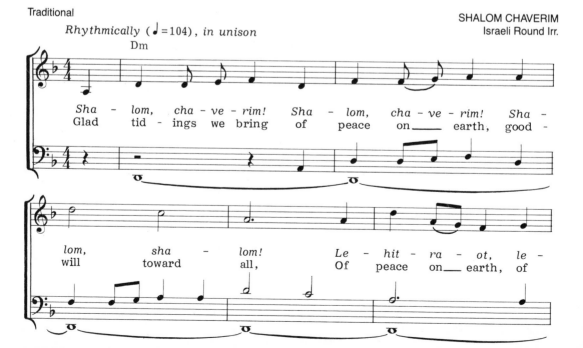

Sha - lom, cha - ve - rim! Sha - lom, cha - ve - rim! Sha -
Glad tid - ings we bring of peace on___ earth, good -

lom, sha - lom! Le - hit - ra - ot, le -
will toward all, Of peace on___ earth, of

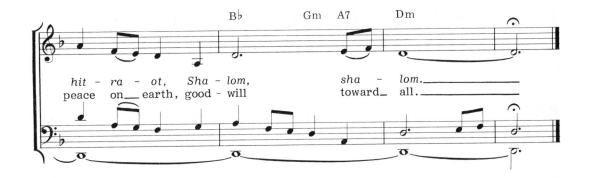

hit - ra - ot, Sha - lom, sha - lom._____
peace on__ earth, good - will toward__ all._____

By the Babylonian Rivers 166

Psalm 137
Ewald Bash, 1964
Altered, 1983

Latvian Melody
Arr. by Ewald Bash, 1964
Harm. by Paul Abels, 1966

Unhurried (♩=92), in unison

1. By the Bab - y - lo - nian riv - ers We sat
2. There our cap - tors in de - ri - sion Did re -
3. How__ shall we sing our God's song In a
4. Let your cross be ben - e - dic - tion For those

down in grief and wept; Hanged our harps up - on a
quire of us a song; So we sat with star - ing
strange and bit - ter land? Can our voic - es veil the
bound in tyr - an - ny; By the power of res - ur -

wil - low, Mourned for Zi - on when we slept.
vi - sion, And the days were hard and long.
sor - row? O God, help your lone - ly band.
rec - tion Loose them from cap - tiv - i - ty.

This song of liberation laments the captivity in Babylon as found in Psalm 137, but goes on to express the hope for freedom from captivity, as the resurrection faith proclaims.

167 Live into Hope of Captives Freed

Luke 4:18–19
Jane Parker Huber, 1976

TRURO L.M.
Thomas Williams' *Psalmodia Evangelica,* 1789

Joyfully (♩ = 138)

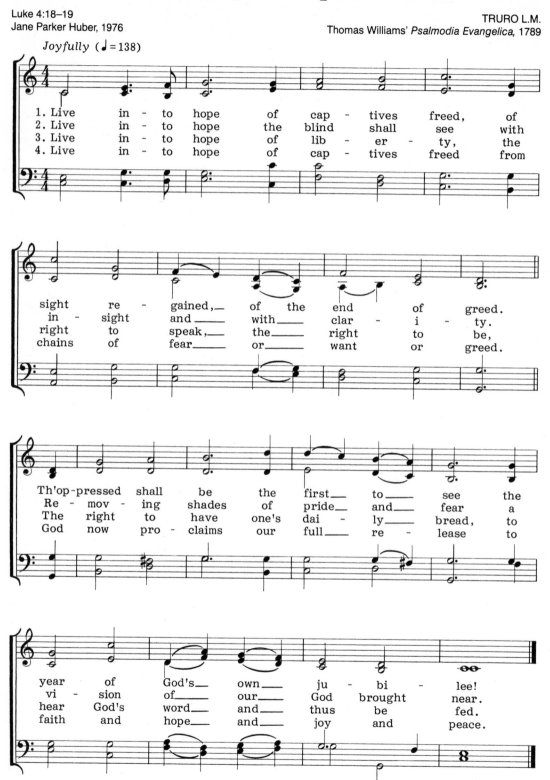

1. Live in-to hope of cap - tives freed, of
2. Live in-to hope the blind shall see with
3. Live in-to hope of lib - er - ty, the
4. Live in-to hope of cap - tives freed from

sight re - gained,— of the end of greed.
in - sight and— with— clar - i - ty.
right to speak,— the— right to be,
chains of fear— or— want or greed.

Th'op-pressed shall be the first— to— see the
Re - mov - ing shades of pride— and— fear a
The right to have one's dai - ly— bread, to
God now pro - claims our full— re - lease to

year of God's— own— ju - bi - lee!
vi - sion of— our— God brought near.
hear God's word— and— thus be fed.
faith and hope— and— joy and peace.

"Truro" is an anonymous melody which was first published in 1789 in Thomas Williams' collection of psalm and hymn tunes for "Churches, Chapels and Dissenting Meetings in England, Scotland and Ireland."

Brothers and Sisters of Mine Are the Hungry 168

Kenneth I. Morse
Altered, 1983

BROTHERS AND SISTERS 11.11.11.11.
Wilbur E. Brumbaugh

1. Broth-ers and sis-ters of mine are the hun-gry Who sigh in their
2. Stran-gers and neigh-bors, they claim my at-ten-tion; They sleep by my
3. Peo-ple are they, men and wom-en and chil-dren; And each has a
4. God of all liv-ing, we make our con-fes-sion: Too long we have

sor-row and weep in their pain. Sis-ters and broth-ers of
door-step, they sit by my bed. Neigh-bors and stran-gers, their
heart keep-ing time with my own. Peo-ple are they, per-sons
wast-ed the wealth of our lands. God of all lov-ing, re-

mine are the home-less Who wait with-out shel-ter from wind and from rain.
an-guish con-cerns me, And I must not feast till the hun-gry are fed.
made in God's im-age; So what shall I of-fer them, bread or a stone?
new our com-pas-sion And o-pen our hearts while we reach out our hands.

169 If We're Going to Walk Together

R. Tiffany Bates

R. Tiffany Bates

we're going to walk_ to - geth - er, if we're going to hike_ to the
we're going to love_ each oth - er, if we're going to join_ hand in
now is the time to start walk - ing and now is the time_ for the

stars,   If we're going to walk for the hun - gry we'd
hand,   If we're going to share with our neigh - bors we'd
song;   To - day is the time__ for lov - ing, we'd

170 Make Us, God, Apostles of Your Peace

Darrell Faires, Sr.

Darrell Faires, Sr.

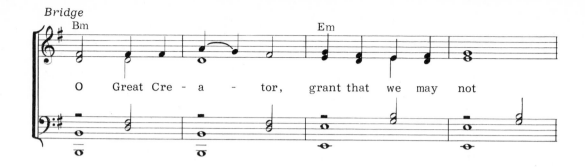

O Great Cre - a - tor, grant that we may not

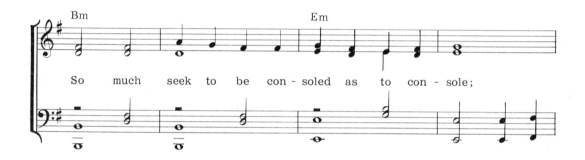

So much seek to be con - soled as to con - sole;

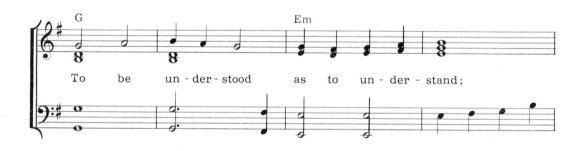

To be un - der - stood as to un - der - stand;

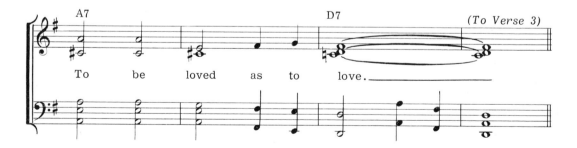

To be loved as to love.

Darrell Faires, Sr. is a Disciples of Christ minister, composer, and performer of his songs.

We Are People of God's Peace

Menno Simons, 1552 "Reply to False Accusations"
Tr. by David Augsburger

NEW COMMUNITY 7.7.7.7.7.7.7.7.
Jan Roh, 1544
Bohemian Brethren

171

Not too fast (♩ =112)
(♩ =one beat)

1. We are peo-ple of God's peace in the new com-mu-ni-ty.
2. We are chil-dren of God's peace in the new com-mu-ni-ty.
3. We are ser-vants of God's peace in the new com-mu-ni-ty.

We are lov-ing, liv-ing peace in the new hu-man-i-ty.
We are car-ing, shar-ing peace in God's lov-ing fam-i-ly.
We are priz-ing, choos-ing peace in God's king-dom faith-ful-ly.

We are daugh-ters of God's peace: we are sons who love God's peace.
Meek, we gen-tly seek for peace: weak, we strong-ly speak for peace.
Je-sus Christ, the Prince of peace, gives us con-fi-dence and peace.

Joined as one to cov-'nant peace in the new com-mu-ni-ty.
Strike, we turn the cheek for peace in the new com-mu-ni-ty.
Christ is our de-fense for peace in the new com-mu-ni-ty.

The writer of these words, Menno Simons, was an Anabaptist leader who emphasized the importance of community and restoring the New Testament life to the church. The Anabaptists' hope was for peace in the world.

172 Dona Nobis Pacem

Traditional Latin

Traditional Round

The Latin phrase means, "Grant us peace," This song may be sung as a round.

173 Let People Living in All Lands

Kenneth L. Patton, 1956
Altered, 1983

VOM HIMMEL HOCH L.M.
Geistliche Lieder, Leipzig, 1539

Let peo-ple liv-ing in all lands De-clare that fear and

Words as altered by permission of the author.

war are done—Joined by the la - bor of___ their hands,

In love and un - der - stand - ing, one.

O God of Love, O God of Peace 174

Henry W. Baker, 1861
Altered, 1983

HESPERUS L.M.
Henry W. Baker, 1821–1877

Gently moving (♩ = 108)

1. O God of love, O God of peace, Make wars through-
2. Re - mem - ber, now your works of old, The won - ders
3. Whom shall we trust but you, O God? Where rest but

out the world to cease; The wrath of sin - ful ones re -
that our fore - bears told; Re - mem - ber not our sin's dark
on your faith - ful word? None ev - er called on you in

strain: Give peace, O God,___ give peace a - gain!
stain: Give peace, O God,___ give peace a - gain!
vain: Give peace, O God,___ give peace a - gain!

175   There's a World Out There

Darrell Faires, Sr.

Darrell Faires, Sr.

176
God, Teach Us Peacemaking

Jane Parker Huber

SLANE 10.10.9.10.
Irish Melody
Harm. by David Evans, 1874–1948

Moderately (♩=76), in unison

1. God, teach us___ peace - mak - ing, jus - tice and love.
2. God, teach us___ peace - mak - ing in church and home,
3. God, teach us___ peace - mak - ing in ev - 'ry role.
4. God, teach us___ peace - mak - ing un - to the end;

Blessed by Christ's teach - ing, we're lift - ed a - bove
In school and gov - ern - ment or where we roam,
In each re - la - tion - ship make peace our goal.
Par - ent or child, or as stran - ger or friend,

All thought_ of___ venge - ance or en - vy or hate.___
In shop___ and___ in - dus - try, cit - y and farm___
Yet give___ us___ in - sight that keeps us a - ware,___
Fill all___ our___ hearts with the pow'r of sha - lom,___

Help us, Your chil - dren, sha - lom to cre - ate.
Show us the path - ways that___ cause no one harm.
Jus - tice and mer - cy in___ bal - ance to share.
Liv - ing to - geth - er, the___ world as our home.

This Is My Song

177

St. 1, 2: Lloyd Stone, 1912
St. 3: Georgia Harkness, adapt., 1983

FINLANDIA 10.10.10.10.10.10.
Jean Sibelius, 1865–1957

1. This is my song, O God of all the na-tions,— A song of
2. My coun-try's skies are blu-er than the o-cean,— And sun-light
3. This is my prayer, O God of all earth's king-doms,— Your king-dom

peace for lands a-far and mine.— This is my home, the
beams on clo-ver-leaf and pine.— But oth-er lands have
come; on earth your will be done.— Let Christ be lift-ed

coun-try where my heart is;— Here are my hopes, my dreams, my ho-ly
sun-light too, and clo-ver,— And skies are ev-'ry-where as blue as
up till all shall serve him,— And hearts u-nit-ed learn to live as

shrine;— But oth-er hearts in oth-er lands are beat-ing—
mine.— So hear my song, O God of all the na-tions,—
one.— So hear my prayer, O God of all the na-tions.—

With hopes and dreams as true and high as mine.—
A song of peace for their land and for mine.—
My-self I give you let your will be done.—

This harmonization of Jean Sibelius' famous melody is from his tone poem and is a composite of the versions in *The Church Hymnary, Revised,* 1927, *The Hymnal* (Presbyterian), 1933, and the composer's piano score for the composition.

Index of Authors, Translators, and Sources

Index of Composers, Arrangers, and Sources

Index of Tunes

Index of First Lines